WASHINGTON, DC

RON BURKE
SUSAN BURKE

Top 10 Washington, DC Highlights

The Top 10 of Everything

CONTENTS

Washington, DC Area by Area

Streetsmart

Within each Top 10 list in this book, no hierarchy of quality or popularity is implied. All 10 are, in the editor's opinion, of roughly equal merit.

Throughout this book, floors are referred to in accordance with American usage; i.e., the "first floor" is at ground level.

Front cover and spine *The monumental US Capitol with the Reflecting Pool at its base*
Back cover *Pedal boats on the Tidal Basin with Thomas Jefferson Memorial in the background*
Title page *The imposing marble statue of Abraham Lincoln in the Lincoln Memorial*

Welcome to
Washington, DC

City of politics and power. City of intrigue, passion, and history. World-renowned museums and monuments, broad avenues, vast green spaces, and breathtaking architecture combine to make this one of the most beautiful, captivating, and fun-to-explore cities in the world. With Eyewitness Top 10 Washington, DC, it's yours to explore.

What's not to love in a city where so much, including 19 Smithsonian museums and galleries, along with scores of monuments, memorials, and even government buildings, is open to the public free of charge? Everyone starts at the **National Mall**, the museum-and-monument-filled park that's the heart of the capital. You'll be able to discover dinosaurs and diamonds at the **National Museum of Natural History**; peruse Monets and Rembrandts in the **National Gallery of Art**; be moved by great words at the **Lincoln Memorial**; and see the city at your feet from the top of the **Washington Monument**.

Beyond the Mall, a cornucopia of theater, shopping, and adventure awaits you – from the legendary performances of the **Kennedy Center**, to the elegant boutiques of **Georgetown**, to the nightlife of **U Street** and **Adams Morgan**. And, of course, when you are ready to eat, you'll find the city overflowing with excellent restaurants serving international and local cuisines for every budget and palate.

Whether you're coming for a weekend or a week, our Top 10 guide brings together the best of everything that Washington, DC has to offer. The guide gives you useful tips throughout, from seeking out what's free to avoiding the crowds, plus six easy-to-follow itineraries, designed to tie together a clutch of sights in a short space of time. Add inspiring photography and detailed maps, and you've got the essential pocket-sized travel companion. **Enjoy the book, and enjoy Washington, DC.**

Clockwise from top: **Jefferson Memorial, Washington Monument**, the North Apse in the Basilica of the National Shrine of the Immaculate Conception, the South Lawn of the White House, Martin Luther King, Jr. Memorial, quote from Franklin Delano Roosevelt Memorial, Georgetown row houses, Lincoln Memorial

Exploring Washington, DC

Whether you have just a couple of days, or more time to explore, there's so much to see and do in America's capital city that you will want to make every minute count. The city is easy to get around on foot, with the Metrorail a fast and efficient alternative. Here are some ideas for how to make the most of your time.

The White House is the residence of the president, as well as the seat of executive power.

Key
- Two-day itinerary
- Four-day itinerary

Two Days in Washington, DC

Day ❶
MORNING
Start at the **National Air and Space Museum** (see pp20–21), then head to the **National Gallery of Art** (see pp24–7). Lunch at **Pavilion Café** (see p91) by the National Sculpture Garden.

AFTERNOON
Walk to the **White House** (see pp16–19) then stroll south to the **Washington Monument** (see p87), then west to the **Lincoln Memorial** (see p86) and the **Jefferson Memorial** (see p88). In the evening head to the **Kennedy Center** (see p99).

Day ❷
MORNING
Start at the **National Museum of Natural History** (see pp28–9) then go next door to the **National Museum of American History** (see pp22–3).

AFTERNOON
Head to the Visitor Center of the **US Capitol** (see pp12–15) and take the Capitol tour, followed by a amble through the lush tropical landscapes within the **US Botanic Garden Conservatory** (see p80). Visit **Penn Quarter** (see p97) for dinner, then join the crowds ambling in the Mall to see the monuments lit up at night.

Four Days in Washington, DC

Day ❶
MORNING
Find out about the nation's story at the **National Museum of American History** (see pp22–3). Then stroll east on the Mall to the **National Gallery of Art** (see pp24–7) and have lunch in the **Cascade Café** (see p91).

AFTERNOON
Take the guided tour of the **Library of Congress** (see p79). Then head to the Visitor Center of the **US Capitol** (see pp12–15), and get a ticket for the tour.

**The National Museum
of Natural History**
captivates visitors,
especially children,
with its lively exhibits.

The Library of Congress
is the largest in the world,
housing over 120 million
items in grand style.

Day ❷
MORNING
Visit the **National Air and Space
Museum** *(see pp20–21)* early to avoid
the crowds. Cross the Mall to the
National Museum of Natural History
(see pp28–9). Have lunch at **Mitsitam
Café** in the **National Museum of the
American Indian** *(see p85)*.
AFTERNOON
Visit the **White House** *(see pp16–19)*,
then head south to the **Washington
Monument** *(see p87)*, then past the
Vietnam Veterans Memorial *(see p86)*
to the **Lincoln Memorial** *(see p86)*
and **Jefferson Memorial** *(see p88)*.

Day ❸
MORNING
Explore **Mount Vernon** *(see pp36–9)*.
Be sure to leave time to visit George
Washington's grist mill and distillery.

AFTERNOON
Spend the afternoon at **Arlington
National Cemetery** *(see pp34–5)*.
Head to **Old Town Alexandria** *(see
p111)* for dinner.

Day ❹
MORNING
Early morning when the animals are
active is the best time to explore the
National Zoological Park *(see pp32–3)*.
Then visit **the National Cathedral**
(see pp30–31) for a tour. Pause for
lunch at **Two Amys** *(see p115)*.
AFTERNOON
Head to **Georgetown** *(see pp104–7)*,
stopping to explore the gorgeous
gardens at **Dumbarton Oaks** *(see
p105)*. Then a short walk leads to
great shopping at **M Street and
Wisconsin Avenue** *(see p105)*. Finish
with dinner at formal **1789** *(see p109)*.

Top 10 Washington, DC Highlights

The US flag flying in front of the United States Capitol

🔟 Washington, DC Highlights

The political, cultural, and spiritual heart of the United States, Washington, DC dazzles its visitors with stirring icons, noble monuments, and magnificent museums at every turn. A selection of the best the city has to offer is explored in the following chapter.

US Capitol ①
The design of the US Capitol combines ancient tradition and New World innovation, perfectly invoking the spirit of US democracy (see pp12–15).

② The White House
The most elegant and familiar of all the world's political residences, the White House has witnessed some of the most consequential decisions of modern history (see pp16–19).

③ National Air and Space Museum
Reportedly, this is the second most visited museum in the world. The artifacts within trace one of mankind's greatest quests (see pp20–21).

National Museum of American History ④
A mix of "America's attic" and contemporary exhibits, ranging from political campaign buttons to historic examples of the Star-Spangled Banner (see pp22–3).

⑤ National Gallery of Art
The National Gallery's vast collection makes it one of the greatest art museums in the world (see pp24–7).

6 National Museum of Natural History

There's lots here to fascinate, from the famous Rotunda elephant to the Hope Diamond and the Live Butterfly Pavilion *(see pp28–9).*

7 Washington National Cathedral

Ancient and modern come together in this, the "national house of prayer," from the Gothic architecture to the Space Window *(see pp30–31).*

8 National Zoological Park

Animals from across the world's varied habitats can be seen and studied at this internationally recognized leader in animal care, breeding of endangered species, and public education *(see pp32–3).*

10 Mount Vernon

George Washington's estate and mansion is a perfect example of the gentleman-farmer roots of many of America's founding fathers *(see pp36–9).*

9 Arlington National Cemetery

Four million people each year visit these rolling lawns studded with the headstones of America's war dead. A moving and reflective experience *(see pp34–5).*

🔟 ⭐ United States Capitol

From its elevated site, described as "a pedestal waiting for a monument," the dignified Capitol has stood unwavering as the symbol of the American democractic process (an often rough-and-tumble one) throughout its more than 200-year history. The Capitol's frescoes and art collection qualify it as a notable museum, but its millions of tourists come, above all, to brush shoulders with history, both remembered and in the making.

Plan of the US Capitol

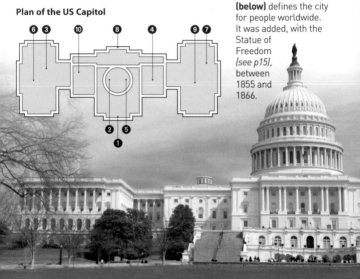

2 Capitol Dome
The central dome **(below)** defines the city for people worldwide. It was added, with the Statue of Freedom *(see p15)*, between 1855 and 1866.

1 Capitol Visitor Center
The vast, underground Visitor Center **(below)** shows videos introducing Congress and the Capitol Complex, while the Exhibition Hall features displays and artifacts that recount the history of the Capitol.

3 Brumidi Corridors
Constantino Brumidi (1805–80) designed these ornate passageways on the lower floor of the Senate wing.

4 National Statuary Hall
The monumental *Liberty and the Eagle* by Enrico Causici (c.1819) over-looks this grand, semi-circular hall. The original House Chamber, it now displays statues of the nation's great and good.

7 Hall of Columns

This striking corridor **(right)**, more than 100 ft (30 m) long with lofty ceilings, is named after the 28 gracefully fluted white marble columns set along its length. It houses additional items from the collection of the original House Chamber.

5 Rotunda

America's first president ascends into the heavens in this 4,664-sq-ft (430-sq-m) fresco *The Apotheosis of Washington*, lining the interior of the monumental dome **(above)**.

8 Columbus Doors

These imposing bronze doors, 17 ft (5 m) tall, are made up of reliefs picturing Christopher Columbus's life and his discovery of America. Designed by Randolph Rogers, the doors were cast in Munich in 1860.

6 Senate Chamber

A semicircle of 100 desks faces the dais in this eminent assembly room. Democrats sit to the right, while Republicans are seated to the left.

9 House Chamber

The largest room in the Capitol is used for daily deliberations of the House of Representatives and for joint meetings of the House and Senate.

10 Old Senate Chamber

Used by the Senate from 1810 to 1859, this fine chamber **(left)** has been the setting for crucial debates on core issues in the development of the United States.

NEED TO KNOW

MAP R5 ■ National Mall, between 1st and 3rd Sts and Constitution and Independence Aves, SW ■ 202-226-8000 ■ www.visitthecapitol.gov

Open 8:30am–4:30pm Mon–Sat; closed on Thanksgiving, Christmas, New Year's Day, and Inauguration Day

Pass required for tours

■ The impressive Visitor Center includes an Exhibition Hall, gift shop, restaurant, and gathering place for tour groups.

■ Security protocols forbid certain items to be carried on tours, including bulky bags and all foods, liquids, and aerosols; check the website for details.

Capitol Guide
Current tours (bookable via the official website) take in all the historic sections in the center of this vast building, including the Rotunda, the National Statuary Hall, and the Crypt. The galleries of the House of Representatives and the Senate are open to the public when either legislative body is in session. Cell phones, cameras, and other forms of recording device are not allowed in the galleries.

Events in the US Capitol's History

1 1791
George Washington selects the site for the new Capitol, with his city planner, Pierre Charles L'Enfant. They chose Jenkins Hill, 88 ft (27 m) above the north bank of the Potomac River.

2 1792
Dr. William Thornton wins a design contest for "Congress House," in which he proposed a simple central domed hall flanked by two rectangular wings.

3 1800
Congress moves from Philadelphia to occupy the north wing of the Capitol.

4 1811
The Capitol is fully occupied by the House of Representatives, Senate, Supreme Court, and Library of Congress.

5 1814
British troops occupy the city and burn many buildings, including the Capitol, during the War of 1812 (which lasted until 1815).

British burn the Capitol in the War of 1812

George Washington

6 1818
Charles Bulfinch takes over the building's restoration and supervises its reconstruction. The Senate House and Supreme Court occupy new rooms by 1819, and the Rotunda is first used in 1824 to host a grand reception for General Lafayette.

7 1851
The Capitol is again damaged by fire. It is redesigned and rebuilt under the direction of Thomas U. Walter, who designs the cast-iron dome. Work continues on the Dome during the Civil War, while the Capitol is also used as a hospital, barracks, and bakery.

8 1880s–1900
Modern electrical lighting and the first elevator are installed. After another fire in 1898, fireproofing was at last added.

9 1958–1962
The east front is extended 32 ft (10 m) east of the old sandstone front. The west front is restored between 1983 and 1987. This work produces the Capitol we see today.

10 2000–2008
The new 580,000 sq ft (53,884 sq m) Capitol Visitor Center, the largest ever expansion of the Capitol, welcomes about three to five million people annually.

Illustration of the US Capitol in 1852

THE STATUE OF FREEDOM

Crowning the Capitol dome stands Thomas Crawford's *Statue of Freedom*, commissioned in 1855. Freedom is depicted as a classical female figure, draped in flowing robes. Her Roman helmet, however, features the crest of an eagle's head, feathers, and talons, which some believe to be a reference to Native American dress. Crawford had originally substituted the Roman helmet for the liberty cap, a symbol of freed slaves, but the then US Secretary of War, Jefferson Davis, objected. The statue faces east in accordance with the front of the building, not, to the puzzlement of many visitors, towards the rest of the nation. The east front was made the main building entrance simply because it faces an approach of level ground. This monumental symbol of liberty is 19.5 ft (6 m) tall and weighs around 15,000 lbs (6,800 kg). Sadly Crawford died in 1857, before it was erected.

The American Ideal
Although the *Statue of Freedom* may appear to face away from the heartland, she is nevertheless the embodiment of all Americans. Standing imperiously over the capital, and the nation as a whole, she encapsulates the notion of freedom for all citizens, laid out in the US Constitution. It is an ideal still fiercely protected today.

TOP 10
WORKS OF ART IN THE US CAPITOL

1 **Statue of Freedom**, Thomas Crawford (Dome)

2 **The Apotheosis of Washington**, Constantino Brumidi (Rotunda)

3 **General George Washington Resigning His Commission**, John Trumball (Rotunda)

4 **Columbus Doors**, Randolph Rogers (East Front)

5 **Minton Tiles** (floors and offices)

6 **Brumidi Corridors** (Senate Wing)

7 **Portrait Monument to Lucretia Mott, Elizabeth Cady Stanton, and Susan B. Anthony, Adelaide Johnson** (Rotunda)

8 **Statuary** (National Statuary Hall), Capitol Visitor Center, and other locations

9 **Declaration of Independence**, John Trumball (Rotunda)

10 **Baptism of Pocahontas, prior to her marriage to John Rolfe**, Antonio Cappellano (Rotunda)

⭐ The White House

Possibly the most famous residential landmark in the world, this dramatic Neo-Classical mansion has been the residence of the US president and family, the seat of executive power, and a working office building for over 200 years. Situated at the nation's most recognizable address, 1600 Pennsylvania Avenue, the White House reflects the power of the presidency. Its 132 rooms preserve and display the cultural settings of America's past and present. Lafayette Park to the north and the Ellipse to the south are good sites for viewing this American icon.

1 North Facade
The stately but welcoming entrance on Pennsylvania Avenue **(below)** has a beautifully proportioned Ionic portico, added in 1829. Painted Virginia sandstone gives the building its white luster.

2 State Dining Room
As many as 140 guests may enjoy the president's hospitality in this formal dining room.

3 South Facade
The large semicircular portico added in 1824 dominates the south view **(right)**. The six main columns create an optical illusion, appearing to stretch from ground to roofline, emphasizing the classical proportions.

4 Map Room
Several graceful Chippendale pieces furnish this private meeting room. Franklin D. Roosevelt adapted it as his situation room to assess the progress of World War II.

5 East Room
The East Room has been used chiefly for large receptions and ceremonial gatherings, such as dances, award presentations, press conferences, banquets, and historic bill and treaty signings.

6 Blue Room
The Blue Room **(below)** is by far the most elegant of all the reception rooms – it was George Washington who suggested its oval shape.

7 Oval Office
Since 1909 this room **(left)** has been the setting for the president's core tasks. Leaders add their own touches – Donald trump added a bust of Winston Churchill along with military and presidential flags behind the Resolute desk.

8 West Wing

This wing is the executive operational center of the White House, moved here in 1902 to allow more privacy in the main building.

9 Lincoln Bedroom

Although the name for this room (below) is a misnomer – Abraham Lincoln actually used it as an office – a number of his possessions are on display here.

10 Visitor Center

The White House Visitor Center (below) has engrossing exhibits on various aspects of the mansion. It also offers park ranger talks, a souvenir shop, and special events such as military band concerts.

NEED TO KNOW

MAP N4 ■ 1600 Pennsylvania Ave, NW (Visitor Center: 1450 Pennsylvania Ave, NW) ■ 202-456-7041 (current information about tours) ■ www.whitehouse.gov

■ If you have a telephoto lens or binoculars, the carved decorations on the north entrance and the Rose Garden, viewed from the Ellipse, deserve your attention.

■ The White House has no public restrooms. The nearest facilities are at the Visitor Center and the Ellipse Visitor Pavilion, near 15th and E streets.

Touring the White House

If you want to tour the White House, you must start the process well before your visit. US citizens must request tickets from their Member of Congress. The request can be made up to three months in advance, but at the very minimum tickets must be requested 21 days in advance. Be aware that tickets are limited and issued on a first come, first served basis. Foreign citizens must make a request for tickets from their embassy in DC.

These self-guided tours are available from 7:30am to 11:30am Tuesdays through Thursdays and 7:30am to 1:30pm Fridays and Saturdays (excluding federal holidays).

For more information, including a list of prohibited items, visit www. whitehouse.gov/ participate/tours-and-events

You can also enjoy a virtual tour of the White House at the White House Visitor Center.

White House Decorative Features

Diplomatic Reception Room

1 Diplomatic Reception Room Wallpaper

The panoramic wallpaper is a set of large "Views of North America" printed in France in 1834.

2 China Room Collection

The White House collection of china services had grown so large by 1917 that Mrs Woodrow Wilson set aside a room in which to display it. Today, state and family china belonging to nearly every US president fills the handsome display cabinets.

3 Lighter Relieving a Steamboat Aground

This 1847 painting in the Green Room, by George Caleb Bingham, conveys the vitality of the nation.

4 Library

This former storage room was turned into a library in 1935, and contains a collection of books intended to reflect the philosophical and practical aspects of the presidency. Many pieces of the furniture in this room are attributed to the cabinet-maker Duncan Phyfe.

5 Monroe Plateau

James Monroe ordered a gilt table service from France in 1817. The plateau centerpiece is an impressive 14.5 ft (4.5 m) long when fully extended.

6 Grand Staircase

Descending to the Central Hall on the north side, the Grand Staircase is used for ceremonial entrances to state events in the East Room. Portraits of 20th-century presidents line the stairwell.

7 The Vermeil Room

"Vermeil" refers to the collection of gilded objects by early 19th-century silversmiths on display. Portraits of several First Ladies adorn the walls, and the room is grounded by one of the Empire-style tables purchased by President Andrew Jackson in 1829 for use in the East Room.

The Vermeil Room

8 Sand Dunes at Sunset, Atlantic City

This beach landscape (c.1885) by Henry Ossawa Tanner was the first work by an African American to be hung in the White House.

9 North Entrance Carvings

Scottish stonemasons created the fine carved surround for the north doorway with flowing garlands of roses and acorns.

Elegant table in the Library

10 Seymour Tall-Case Clock

This Oval Office clock ticks so loudly that its pendulum must be stopped whenever any television broadcasts originate from the room.

PRESIDENT TRUMAN'S RENOVATIONS

Harry S. Truman

On moving into the White House, Harry S. Truman observed: "The floors pop and the drapes move back and forth," and "[t]he damned place is haunted, sure as shootin'." In 1948, after investigation, engineers confirmed that it was structural weakness, not ghosts, that was causing the problems. Some people said the house was standing "only from force of habit." The only solution was to move the First Family out and completely rebuild the White House within its external walls, gutting the inside entirely, and building a steel frame within the shell. Within it, the building was recreated, room by room, from scratch. Most structural elements seen today were built between 1948 and 1952, although a few older elements had been carefully dismantled and re-installed during reconstruction. America's three major networks broadcast the first-ever television tour of the residence in 1952. President Truman himself proudly led the tour and even entertained viewers by playing a tune on one of the pianos in the East Room *(see p16)*. A decade later, that arbiter of style Jacqueline Kennedy again restored many of the period features.

TOP 10
EVENTS IN THE WHITE HOUSE'S HISTORY

1 George Washington supervises construction (1792)

2 John and Abigail Adams move in (1800)

3 The Lewis and Clark expedition to the Northwest is planned (1803)

4 The British burn down the White House (1814)

5 James Monroe moves into the partially rebuilt residence (1817)

6 The Executive Mansion is renamed the "White House" (1901)

7 President Roosevelt's World War II "Fireside Chats" inform and inspire the American public

8 Jackie Kennedy restores the house (1961–2)

9 Richard Nixon announces his resignation (Aug 8, 1974)

10 Barack Obama becomes first African-American President (2009)

The White House was gutted in 1948 and completely rebuilt.

TOP10 ⭐ National Air and Space Museum

This fascinating museum pays homage to some of the most ingenious and beautiful objects of flight, from the Wright brothers' biplane to powerful spacecraft. America by Air tells the story of America's airline industry from the formative years of mechanical flight. Compelling exhibitions put these historic objects in their social and political context.

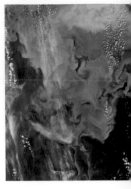

① Moving Beyond Earth

This exhibition explores the history and importance of human spaceflight in the US during the Space Shuttle and International Space Station era, interpreting the story of human spaceflight through artifacts, immersive experiences, and high-tech interactive kiosks.

② 1903 Wright Flyer

On December 17, 1903, Orville Wright flew this twin-winged craft (left) 120 ft (35 m), making it the first powered, piloted plane to be airborne. Muslin on a spruce and ash frame provided a light but strong body. The Wright brothers also designed the engine.

③ How Things Fly

Hands-on exhibits here lead visitors through the basics of flight, both human and animal, and explain forces that control flight of all types, from a helium balloon to a mission to Mars.

④ Looking at Earth

The focus here is on the contribution aerial photography (above) and space flight have given to our understanding of Earth. Many images are breathtakingly beautiful.

⑤ Skylab Orbital Workshop

This gold cylinder was an identical backup to the workshop module that provided living and research space for the first US space station.

⑥ Apollo 11 Command Module Columbia

This vessel was the command center for the first lunar landing. It carried Neil Armstrong, Michael Collins, and "Buzz" Aldrin to the Moon and back.

⑦ WWI and WWII Aviation

A spectacular collection of Allied and Axis planes (left) from World Wars I and II – such as the Messerschmitt Bf 109 and the Supermarine Spitfire – makes this one of the most popular parts of the museum.

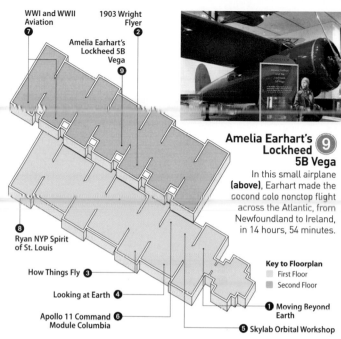

7 WWI and WWII Aviation

2 1903 Wright Flyer

9 Amelia Earhart's Lockheed 5B Vega

8 Ryan NYP Spirit of St. Louis

3 How Things Fly

4 Looking at Earth

6 Apollo 11 Command Module Columbia

Amelia Earhart's Lockheed 5B Vega **9**

In this small airplane **(above)**, Earhart made the second solo nonstop flight across the Atlantic, from Newfoundland to Ireland, in 14 hours, 54 minutes.

Key to Floorplan
- First Floor
- Second Floor

1 Moving Beyond Earth

5 Skylab Orbital Workshop

8 Ryan NYP Spirit of St. Louis

In 1927, Charles Lindbergh flew this plane on the world's first solo trans-atlantic flight, 3,610 miles (5,810 km) from Long Island to Paris. His 33-hour flight made him one of the most famous men of his age. The initials NYP in the plane's name stand for New York–Paris.

10 Steven F. Udvar-Hazy Center

This display and restoration center consists of two exhibition hangars spread across 17 acres (7 ha) near Dulles Airport. Opened to celebrate the 100th anniversary of the Wright brothers' first powered flight, it has nearly 300 aircraft and spacecraft, including the space shuttle *Discovery*.

NEED TO KNOW

MAP Q5 ■ Independence Ave, 6th St, SW ■ 202-633-1000 ■ www.airandspace.si.edu

Open 10am–5:30pm daily; closed Dec 25

Adm required only for planetarium shows and theater screenings: $9 adults, $8 seniors, $7.50 children (2–12 years), $6.50 for members of the Smithsonian

Steven F. Udvar-Hazy Center: 14390 Air and Space Museum Pkwy, Chantilly, VA 20151; 703-572-4118; open 10am–5:30pm daily

■ McDonald's and Wright Place Food Court are in the greenhouse-like extension on the east end of the building.

■ The museum features in *Night at the Museum 2: Battle of the Smithsonian*, starring Ben Stiller (2009).

Museum Guide

Entrances to the museum are on Independence Ave and the Mall. Both lead into the spacious central hall where the most famous airplanes of all time are displayed. An information booth is near the Independence Ave entrance. To see a film at the Lockheed Martin IMAX Theater or the Albert Einstein Planetarium, buy tickets on arrival, or buy them in advance online.

TOP 10 ⭐ National Museum of American History

Three huge floors filled with a variety of fascinating objects make up this paean to American culture. The first floor focuses on science and technology, including hands-on experiments and exhibitions on transport, electricity, and machinery. The second floor is home to the famous Star-Spangled Banner, while the third floor features a stirring tribute to the American presidency and military history.

1 The Price of Freedom: Americans at War
This gallery explores the nation's military history, from the French and Indian War in the 1750s to recent conflicts in Afghanistan and Iraq.

2 American Stories
A collection of wonderful artifacts from the world of popular entertainment, including Dorothy's ruby slippers from *The Wizard of Oz*, Kermit the Frog, and other favorites from the worlds of entertainment and sports.

3 Inventing in America
Well-known inventors Alexander Graham Bell, Samuel Morse, Thomas Edison, and other distinguished members of the National Inventors Hall of Fame feature in this exhibit highlighting past and present innovations. Don't miss the workshop of Ralph Baer, inventor of the home video game.

4 The First Ladies
The First Ladies' gallery is a firm favorite with visitors and includes inaugural gowns worn by Jackie Kennedy, Nancy Reagan, Frances Cleveland **(left)**, Michelle Obama, and many others.

5 FOOD: Transforming the American Table 1950–2000
A meticulous recreation of American chef Julia Child's kitchen **(above)** opens this exploration of the significant changes in the production and consumption of food and wine in postwar America.

6 Gunboat Philadelphia
In October 1776, the *Philadelphia* was sunk by the British during a battle on Lake Champlain on the US–Canadian border, and rested on the bottom of the lake until it was recovered in 1935. It came to the museum in 1964, complete with its equipment and the 24-pound ball that caused the gunboat to sink.

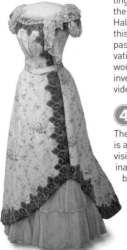

10 Within These Walls...
A two-storey colonial Massachusetts house has been rebuilt in the museum, to explore the 200-year-long history of the families who lived and worked there

7 The Star-Spangled Banner
The flag that inspired the national anthem (above) is strikingly large – originally 30 by 42 ft (9 by 13 m) – although timeworn. Made by Baltimore flag-maker Mary Pickersgill in 1813, it is in a gallery that re-creates the Battle of Baltimore and the burning of the White House.

Key to Floorplan
- First floor
- Second floor
- Third floor

8 America on the Move
Multimedia presentations and other theatrical techniques tell the story of America's transportation since 1876. The vast exhibition holds over 340 objects, such as an 1897 gasoline tricycle.

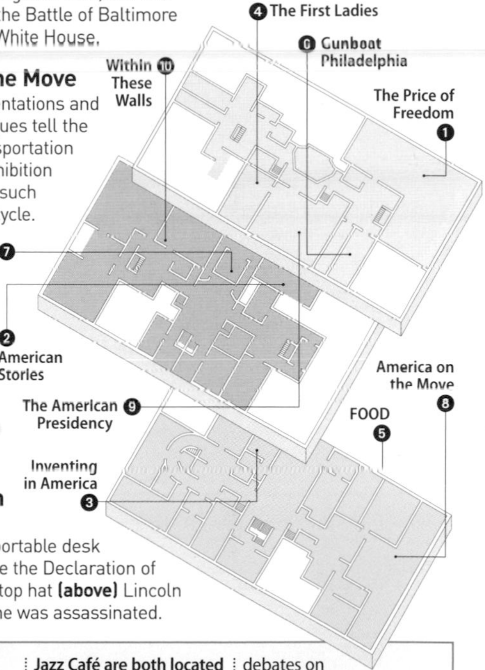

Floorplan labels:
4 The First Ladies
6 Gunboat Philadelphia
The Price of Freedom ❶
Within These Walls ❿
The Star-Spangled Banner ❼
❷ American Stories
The American Presidency ❾
Inventing in America ❸
America on the Move ❽
FOOD ❺

9 The American Presidency
Highlights include the portable desk at which Jefferson wrote the Declaration of Independence, and the top hat (above) Lincoln was wearing the night he was assassinated.

NEED TO KNOW

MAP P4 ■ 14th St and Constitution Ave, NW ■ 202-633-1000 ■ www.americanhistory.si.edu

Open 10am–5:30pm daily; extended hours in summer (check on the website); closed Dec 25

■ The Stars and Stripes Café and LeRoy Neiman

Jazz Café are both located within the museum and offer a variety of dishes.

Museum Events
An amazing variety of events, both entertaining and enlightening, are available to the public. Phone ahead or check online for updates. Try out some of the interactive exhibits, or take part in debates on controversial issues. One highlight is a section of the original Woolworth's lunch counter from Greensboro, NC, a landmark from the Civil Rights Movement, when African-Americans sat at this "whites only" counter asking to be served. At regular intervals you are invited to relive the events of 1960.

TOP 10 ⭐ National Gallery of Art

The collections at this immense gallery rival those of any art museum in the world, displaying milestones of Western art from the Middle Ages to the 20th century and including Italian Renaissance works, Dutch Masters, French Impressionists, and all ages of American art. John Russell Pope designed the harmonious Neo-Classical West Building in 1941.

4 The Adoration of the Magi
This festive view of the Magi at Christ's birthplace **(left)** was painted in tempura on a circular panel by Fra Angelico and Fra Filippo Lippi in about 1445.

5 Watson and the Shark
The dramatic subject matter, muscular painting, and expressions of dread and anxiety meant that this John Singleton Copley painting caused a sensation when it was first displayed in 1778.

1 Calder Mobile, East Building
Alexander Calder's swooping structure, his last major work (set up in 1977), dominates the atrium of the I.M. Pei-designed East Building.

3 Ginevra de' Benci
The modeling of lustrous flesh against juniper make this Leonardo canvas of 1474 – his only one in the Americas – a lively, composed work.

2 The Jolly Flatboatmen
George Caleb Bingham's 1846 masterpiece **(below)** is a realistic depiction of life and work along one of America's largest rivers.

6 Girl with the Red Hat
This 1665 portrait **(above)** shows off Johannes Vermeer's striking use of color: yellow highlights in the blue robe, purple under the hat, turquoise in the eyes. The luminosity is enhanced by the smooth panel base.

9 The River of Light
Frederick Edwin Church's 1877 oil painting of the Amazon is based on sketches taken during a trip to South America. This otherworldly work emphasizes the power of nature.

7 Right and Left
The title of Winslow Homer's 1909 work (above) refers to shooting ducks with separate barrels of a shotgun. The fleeting nature of the ducks' existence echoes our own.

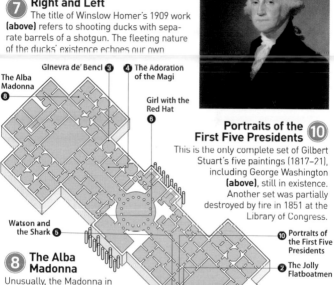

Ginevra de' Benci **3**
The Alba Madonna **8**
4 The Adoration of the Magi
Girl with the Red Hat **6**

Portraits of the First Five Presidents **10**
This is the only complete set of Gilbert Stuart's five paintings (1817–21), including George Washington (above), still in existence. Another set was partially destroyed by fire in 1851 at the Library of Congress.

Watson and the Shark **5**

8 The Alba Madonna
Unusually, the Madonna in Raphael's 1510 work is shown seated on the ground. The composition is serene, but it shows Christ accepting the cross from St. John the Baptist, a precursor of events to come.

10 Portraits of the First Five Presidents
2 The Jolly Flatboatmen
9 El Rio de Luz (The River of Light)
7 Right and Left
1 Calder Mobile, East Building

NEED TO KNOW

MAP Q4 ■ 3rd–9th Sts at Constitution Ave, NW ■ 202-737-4215 ■ www.nga.gov

Open 10am–5pm Mon–Sat, 11am–6pm Sun; closed Dec 25, Jan 1

■ The Cascade Café, set between the West and East Buildings, has an espresso bar, while the Pavilion Café located in the Sculpture Garden is a great spot to grab a bite.

■ The gallery acquired over 8,000 works from the world-renowned Corcoran Gallery of Art, which closed in 2014. Many of these are now on display in the West Building.

Gallery Guide
The main floor contains European paintings and sculpture and American art. The ground floor has works on paper, sculpture, decorative arts, and temporary exhibits. From here, an underground concourse leads to the East Building. Note that the location of works changes periodically.

National Gallery of Art Collections

The Dance Lesson, a 19th-century Impressionist painting by Edgar Degas

1 French 19th-Century Paintings

Especially rich in Impressionist works, this collection includes some of the world's most beloved works of art, such as Monet's *Japanese Footbridge* and Degas' *Four Dancers* and *The Dance Lesson*.

2 American Paintings

The breadth of this collection reveals many interesting themes: portraiture, a desire for accuracy in depicting American life and land-scape, and a social conscience.

3 Italian 13th- to 16th-Century Paintings

Best known for the increasing mastery of the naturalistic portrayal of the human figure and of interior and exterior settings, the works in this extensive collection still have appealing variety: decorative, mystical, simple, and elegant.

4 Italian, French, and Spanish 16th-Century Paintings

The mature flowering of the Renaissance bursts forth in this broad collection of works by Raphael, Giorgione, Titian, and many others.

5 Works on Paper

The gallery is especially strong in this area. Repeat visitors see an almost unbelievable quantity and variety of exquisite drawings, prints, illustrated books, and photographs. The permanent collection contains more than 65,000 items, dating as far back as the 11th century.

6 17th-Century Dutch and Flemish Paintings

Visitors will find an overwhelmingly rich array of Old Master works by artists such as Rembrandt, Frans Hals, Van Dyck, Rubens, Vermeer, and their contemporaries.

7 Spanish Paintings

El Greco, Zurbarán, Murillo, and Velázquez are just some of the 18th- to 19th-century highlights in this vibrant collection.

8 Decorative Arts

Sumptuous tapestries, full of imagery, outstanding pieces of furniture, and everyday items such as Chinese porcelain plates and bowls, give a wonderful glimpse of passing centuries.

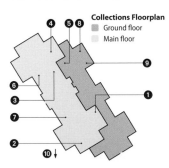

Collections Floorplan
■ Ground floor
■ Main floor

9 European Sculpture

Portrait busts and portrait medals have always been important products of the sculptor's studio, and many fine examples are displayed here. There is also an especially absorbing selection of Rodin's work and some interesting experimental sculptural pieces by Degas.

10 Painting and Sculpture of the 20th Century

Here you can trace the frantic rate of change in 20th-century art, from Matisse's Fauvist works, the Cubists Picasso and Braque, the abstraction of Mondrian, and Surrealists such as Magritte and Miró right up to Minimalism and Pop Art.

THE EAST BUILDING AND SCULPTURE GARDEN

The East Building is an angular construction designed to house permanent and touring exhibitions of contemporary art. Its entrance is from 4th Street or from the underground concourse leading from the West Building. The lobby is dominated by a huge red, black, and blue mobile by Alexander Calder, while exhibition rooms line the outer walls of the upper halls, connected by hanging crosswalks. Following recent renovations, the new fourth floor features an outdoor sculpture terrace and two skylit gallery towers. The Sculpture Garden is a lively public space integrating contemporary art with beautifully landscaped gardens and a relaxing reflection pool with its spraying central fountain. In a 6-acre (2.5-ha) block next to the West Building, the garden has native trees, shrubs, and perennials, along with 18 pieces from the gallery's collection and several items here on loan from other museums. There are free jazz concerts on summer Fridays, and the pool transforms into a popular ice-skating rink in winter.

Seating in the Sculpture Garden

TOP 10 ⊛ National Museum of Natural History

From the earrings of Marie Antoinette to the giant jaws of a prehistoric shark, this museum is full of fascinating treasures collected by Smithsonian scientists for over a century. Ancient mummies, rare gems and minerals, previously unknown plants and animals, and the bones of mighty dinosaurs are on display, making this one of the most popular museums on the Mall.

3 African Elephant

This huge bull elephant **(left)** seems to fill the Rotunda and has become a symbol of the museum itself. Weighing in at over 8 tons, this was the largest land animal on display when it was unveiled in 1959. Exhibits tell the story of African elephants and the threats they face today.

4 Fossil Lab

Look through the windows into a genuine fossil lab where museum scientists clean, prepare, and mount fossils from around the world that have recently been collected by scientists.

5 Live Insect Zoo

All kinds of insects can be viewed in their natural habitats here. Volunteers do tarantula feedings and offer children a chance to touch and hold live insects each day.

1 Hope Diamond

Not the world's largest diamond, but certainly the most famous, and possibly the most viewed artifact in any museum in the world. The 45.52 carat deep-blue diamond **(left)** was part of the French Crown Jewels, and is reputed to be cursed.

2 The Last American Dinosaur

The museum's legendary National Fossil Hall is undergoing reconstruction until 2019. In the meantime, dinosaur fans can view this special exhibit that highlights the large dinosaurs that roamed the earth just before a global catastrophe ended their reign.

6 Hall of Mammals

From a roaring African lion **(above)** to an enormous Grizzly Bear standing on its hind legs, this hall is filled with dramatic representations of warm-blooded animals from around the world.

7 Live Butterfly Pavilion

A family favorite, this pavilion lets you stroll among fluttering beauties with fanciful names like Gulf Fritillary (left) and Madagascar Moon Moth.

8 Ptolemaic Mummy

This mummy of a 40-year-old man who died over 2,000 years ago is the star of "Eternal Life in Ancient Egypt." Displays include a step-by-step guide to the process of mummification.

ORIGINS OF THE SMITHSONIAN

The world's largest museum complex, the Smithsonian Institute was founded in 1826 when British scientist James Smithson left half a million dollars (about $15 million today) "to found in Washington, under the name of the Smithsonian Institution, an establishment for the increase and diffusion of knowledge among men." Today, the Smithsonian Institute in Washington comprises 19 museums, 9 research centers, and a zoo, and every one of its public venues can be entered free of charge.

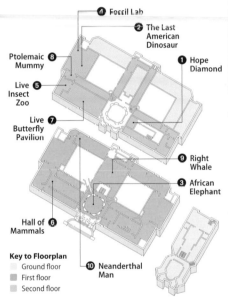

- 4 Fossil Lab
- 2 The Last American Dinosaur
- 1 Hope Diamond
- 8 Ptolemaic Mummy
- 5 Live Insect Zoo
- 7 Live Butterfly Pavilion
- 9 Right Whale
- 3 African Elephant
- 6 Hall of Mammals
- 10 Neanderthal Man

Key to Floorplan
- Ground floor
- First floor
- Second floor

9 Right Whale

The life-size model hanging from the ceiling of the impressive Hall of Oceans is of a real whale named Phoenix that the Smithsonian has tracked since 1987.

10 Neanderthal Man

The result of painstaking forensic and reconstruction work, this life-size head is one of many artifacts exploring the evolution of humans.

NEED TO KNOW

MAP P4 ■ 10th St and Constitution Ave, NW ■ 202-633-1000 ■ www.naturalhistory.si.edu

Open 10am–5:30pm daily; closed Dec 25; the National Fossil Hall is closed for major renovation work until 2019

Adm by timed ticket to the Live Butterfly Pavilion (free Tue); book online

■ The Atrium Café offers locally sourced vegetables and hormone-free meats, in the form of burgers, pizzas, deli sandwiches, and other family-pleasing meals. Café Natural offers coffee drinks, ice cream, and desserts.

■ Teens, tweens, and children will enjoy Q?rius (pronounced "curious"), an interactive learning space connecting science with everyday life and offering young people a new way to discover the natural world. Visit qrius.si.edu for opening hours.

■ If you want a quieter museum experience, it's a good idea to plan on visiting from Monday to Wednesday. Saturday is usually the busiest day of the week.

TOP 10 ⭐ Washington National Cathedral

This Gothic building is the focus of public spiritual life. The sixth largest cathedral in the world, it was completed in 1990, with a 10-storey-high nave and a central tower 676 ft (206 m) tall, the highest point in the District of Columbia. This Episcopal church is officially named the Cathedral Church of Saint Peter and Saint Paul.

① South Rose Window

"The Church Triumphant" is the theme of this elegant stained-glass rose window **(right)**. The design of Joseph G. Reynolds incorporates 12 brilliantly colored "petals" and numerous other figures. It is mirrored by the North Rose window.

② Space Window

This stained-glass window by artist Rodney Winfield is notable for commemorating mankind's 20th-century moon landing. A piece of moon rock, brought back by Apollo 11 astronauts, is embedded in it.

③ Exterior

The architecture of the cathedral is predominantly English Gothic, created using authentic methods dating from the Middle Ages, including a cross-shaped floorplan, flying buttresses, and spired towers **(right)**.

④ Pipe Organ

This magnificent Aeolian-Skinner instrument has 10,647 pipes. On most Mondays and Wednesdays at 12:30pm, an organist gives visitors a presentation and then demonstrates with a mini-recital.

⑤ Nave

The vertical impression given by the nave **(left)** is also typical of English Gothic style. Flags of the states are often displayed around the outer walls.

⑥ Main Entrance and Creation

The west entrance is centered within a high Gothic arch containing a lovely rose window. Sited above the huge bronze double doors is *Ex Nihilo*, a relief by 20th-century American sculptor Frederick Hart, which portrays the creation of humankind from chaos.

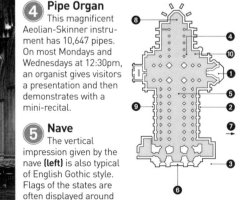

Cathedral floorplan

7 Gardens

A medieval walled garden is the model for the cathedral's beautiful Bishop's Garden **(right)** on the south side of the church. The herb gardens are a delight to the nose as well as the eye. All the stones here originated in a quarry that George Washington once owned.

BUILDING THE CATHEDRAL

In 1893, Congress granted a charter to construct Washington National Cathedral. Theodore Roosevelt attended the laying of the foundation stone at the Mount St. Albans location in 1907. The stone was brought from a field near Bethlehem. The completion of the west towers in 1990 marked the end of 83 years of ceaseless work. In 2011, the cathedral was severely damaged by an earthquake and works to restore the structure continue.

8 High Altar

The imposing high altar at the east end of the magnificent nave is made from stone dug from Solomon's quarry outside Jerusalem.

NEED TO KNOW

MAP H4 ■ Massachusetts & Wisconsin Aves, NW ■ 202-537-6200 ■ www.cathedral.org

Open 10am–5:30pm Mon–Fri, 10am–4pm Sat, 7:45am–4pm Sun (weekend hours subject to change); worship at 8am; tours begin at 12:45

Adm $12 adults; $8 senior citizens & youth 5–17yrs; free under 5 yrs & for services and worship

■ The cathedral offers live music concerts year-round.

■ Binoculars or a telephoto lens are a must for appreciating the gargoyles and grotesques.

9 Gargoyles and Grotesques

Derived from decorated spouts on European buildings, these carved ornaments have been given free rein at the cathedral. The 112 carvings include Darth Vader and a predatory-looking snake.

10 Children's Chapel

This endearing room is child-scaled, with a miniature organ and altar and chairs to fit six-year-olds. Jesus is also shown as a boy in the sculpture here.

TOP 10 ⭐ National Zoological Park

Opened in 1889, and one of the most visited destinations in Washington, the Smithsonian's National Zoo is a beautifully landscaped 163-acre (66-ha) urban park and an innovative center for animal care and conservation. Children and adults delight at seeing rare giant pandas, endangered Asian elephants, and majestic tigers. More than 2,000 animals live here, increasingly housed in habitats that allow natural behavior.

Great Cats ①
The endangered Sumatran tiger has been successfully bred at the National Zoo. Nearby are lions, caracals, and cheetahs **(right)**; visit the Asia Trail to see leopards and Southeast Asian fishing cats.

③ **Giant Pandas**
Mei Xiang and Tian Tian, two giant pandas **(left)** on loan from China, made their first appearance at the zoo in 2001 as part of a research and conservation program. Their male cub Bei Bei was born at the National Zoo in 2015 and will be moved to China before he is four years old.

④ **Cheetah Conservation Station**
Cheetahs and zebras (separated by a fence) display natural behaviors in a grassland setting shared with gazelles and other African savanna-dwellers.

⑤ **American Bison**
Zora and Wilma came here from the American Prairie Preserve in 2014 as part of the zoo's 125th anniversary celebration. Here, they forage, roam and rest in their prairie grasslands habitat.

② **Reptile Discovery Center**
The center's 70 reptile and amphibian species include snakes, turtles, frogs, and the Komodo dragon, a venomous Indonesian lizard that can grow as large as 200 lbs (90 kg) and 10 ft (3 m) long.

NEED TO KNOW

MAP J4 ■ 3001 Connecticut Ave, NW ■ 202-633-4888 ■ www.nationalzoo.si.edu

Open mid-Mar–Oct: grounds 8am–7pm, buildings 9am–6pm daily; Nov–mid-Mar: grounds 8am–5pm, buildings 9am–4pm daily; closed Dec 25

■ The Snore and Roar sleepover between June and September allows visitors to take a nocturnal tour and camp overnight in the zoo.

■ Most children's tour groups arrive between 10am and noon in the fall. Visit the giant pandas after 2pm.

Map of the National Zoological Park

8 Great Apes
Western lowland gorillas **(left)** are among our closest relatives, sharing about 98 percent of our genes. Their movements and human-like manner mesmerize observers. The primates are outdoors in the mornings and mid-afternoons.

9 Asian Elephants
One of the most popular exhibits at the zoo is Elephant Trails. This state-of-the-art enclosure recreates the elephants' natural home, featuring unique outdoor and indoor habitats.

6 Asia Trail
This trail is home to sloth bears, clouded leopards, fishing cats, otters, red pandas, a Japanese giant salamander, and giant pandas.

ZOO HORTICULTURE
The zoo's lush parklands are far more than just pleasant surroundings. In the Elephant Trails habitat, for example, tall trees offer shade, pools support swimming and bathing, and elephants can walk along a 440-yd (400-m) trail. In the Cheetah Conservation Station, the big cats can roam a re-creation of their native habitats.

7 Kids' Farm
Home to alpacas, cows, donkeys, and goats, plus some rare breeds, this exhibit gives children the opportunity to pet and groom the animals. There is also a giant playground for kids to let off steam.

10 Amazonia
This exhibit **(above)** recreates the tropical habitat of the Amazon basin and features a variety of animals, including poison arrow frogs, titi monkeys, and a two-toed sloth.

⭐ Arlington National Cemetery

Some of America's most cherished burial sites are found in the nation's best-known military cemetery. The rolling lawns filled with white tombstones, the Tomb of the Unknowns, and the grave of John F. Kennedy are conspicuous symbols of sacrifices made for freedom. The flags fly at half-staff from before the first and after the last of 27–30 funerals per day, as the graves of veterans continue to multiply. Nearly four million people visit the cemetery every year.

1 Lawns of Graves
More than 400,000 people are buried on these grounds, marked by simple graves, arranged in regular grids, spread across the lawns **(right)**. Although only a small percentage of America's war dead lie here, the expanse gives a tangible picture of the human cost of war.

4 Memorial Amphitheater
This marble amphitheater **(left)** is the setting for the Memorial Day, Easter, and Veterans' Day ceremonies *(see p73)*, when the nation's leaders pay tribute to those who have served their country.

2 Confederate Memorial
Although the cemetery is often thought to be only for Union soldiers, 482 Confederate soldiers are buried here too, around a central memorial.

3 Tomb of Pierre L'Enfant
Honoring the designer of the Washington city grid *(see p42)*, L'Enfant's monument shows his magnificent plan of the city within a circle.

5 Arlington House
This impressive mansion was conceived as a memorial to George Washington, built by his adopted grandson.

6 Tomb of the Unknowns
This monument **(right)** is guarded 24 hours a day by the Old Guard. Unknown soldiers of World Wars I and II and the Korean War lie here. A Vietnam soldier was interred here, but he was later identified.

7 Rough Riders Memorial

This granite memorial **(left)** displays the insignia of the First US Volunteer Cavalry (the "Rough Riders") and the battles they fought during the Spanish–American War.

8 Seabees Memorial

A bronze construction worker pauses to help a young child. The Seabees (the Construction Battalion) performed daring feats in building the military bases needed to win World War II.

9 Shuttle Memorials

One memorial honors the astronauts who died in the space shuttle *Challenger* disaster in 1986. Another nearby is to the crew lost in the 2003 *Columbia* shuttle tragedy.

10 Grave of John F. Kennedy

The eternal flame next to the grave **(above)** of the assassinated president was lit by Jacqueline Kennedy on the day of his funeral. In 1994, she was buried beside him.

Map of the Cemetery

NEED TO KNOW

MAP K6 ▪ Arlington, VA ▪ 877-907-8585
▪ www.arlingtoncemetery.mil

Open Apr–Sep: 8am–7pm daily; Oct–Mar: 8am–5pm daily

▪ The ANC tour bus departs from the Welcome Center throughout the day. The interpretative tour includes stops at major sites. Tickets cost $13.50 for adults, $6.75 for children (4–12), $10 for seniors (65 years and over); free shuttle to graves.

▪ The Welcome Center has a bookstore, restrooms, and water fountains.

🔟 ⭐ Mount Vernon

This graceful mansion, on the banks of the Potomac River, is the second most visited historic residence in America after the White House. George Washington inherited the estate aged 22, and lived at Mount Vernon for over 40 years. With many of the buildings and activities brought back to life, no other place better portrays the character of the first US president, or the role of slavery-based agriculture in the young republic.

6 New Room
This impressive two-storey room (below) is formal enough for state business yet inviting to all. For a table, Washington used boards placed on trestles – easier to clear away for post-dinner dancing.

1 Mansion's Exterior
The huge portico (above) overlooking the Potomac was the president's own design. The house is made of pine, but the exterior was "rusticated" with a treatment that re-creates the look of weathered stone.

4 West Parlor
This charming parlor was one of George Washington's favorite rooms, and he had it decorated in stylish Prussian blue paint, with an English Wilton carpet. A portrait of him, by artist Charles Willson Peale, hangs here.

2 Nelly Custis Bedroom
Martha Washington's granddaughter, Nelly Custis, lived at Mount Vernon from early childhood. This comfortable room was hers; she even stayed here for a short while after she had married.

5 Master Bedroom
This room, often known as Mrs. Washington's Room, is where George and Martha slept. The oversized mahogany bed was ordered by Martha in the 1790s.

3 Little Parlor
Many visitors find this pretty room (right) a highlight of the mansion because it reflects the family life lived in the house. The original harpsichord Washington purchased for his step-granddaughter, Nelly Custis, is displayed.

9 Kitchen

Mrs. Washington directed a staff of slaves in the kitchen **(left)**, with the names of two cooks known today: Nathan and Lucy. Much physical labor was required for cooking – all the fuel and water had to be hauled in by hand.

7 Lafayette Bedroom

This guest bedroom, with its beautiful view of the Potomac, is one of five and is where the Marquis de Lafayette, one of Washington's military aides and a lifelong friend, would stay.

10 Study

This room was the setting for Washington's commercial, political, and public work. It was also his dressing room, where he would wash and shave, and a place of retreat from the bustle of the household.

BUILDING MOUNT VERNON

The estate that was to be Mount Vernon had been in the Washington family since 1674. George Washington inherited the estate in 1754 and in the succeeding years built up the property and grounds. Additions to the house were already underway at the start of the Revolutionary War, but the house's dining room was completed only after the war.

NEED TO KNOW

3200 Mount Vernon Memorial Highway ■ 703-780-2000 ■ www. mountvernon.org

Open Apr–Oct: 9am–5pm daily; Nov–Mar: 9am–4pm daily

Adm $20 adults; $19 senior citizens; $10 children 6–11 years; free under 6 yrs

■ Re-enactments are held throughout the year. See website for details and dates.

■ The Mount Vernon shops sell seeds of some of the estate's heritage plants, as well as gardening books detailing their care.

■ Outside the main entrance is a complex with a full-service restaurant, the Mount Vernon Inn, which offer specialties such as peanut and chestnut soup and salmon corncakes, as well as a food court which serves snacks and quick eats.

Key to Floorplan
- First floor
- Second floor
- Third floor

8 Cupola

The cupola, with its "dove-of-peace" weathervane, provides light to the third floor and aids air circulation in summer.

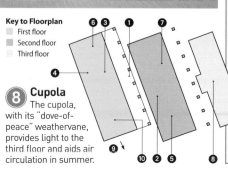

Mount Vernon Grounds

The reconstructed 16-sided treading barn in Mount Vernon Grounds

1 16-Sided Treading Barn

With this unique design, George Washington created one of the most aesthetically pleasing yet efficient working barns. The building's circular plan with its slatted upper floor allowed horses to tread over grain placed on the floor, which separated the heads from the stalks. The grain then fell through the slats into temporary storage below. The building seen today is a painstaking reconstruction of the original based on thorough research by numerous archeologists and curators.

Shipping and Receiving Dock

2 Shipping and Receiving Dock

The wharf of the plantation was the main transportation center for shipping outbound produce and receiving farming and household supplies. The Potomac River was a major carrier of passengers and trade goods in Washington's day. At this evocative spot on its banks, it is easy to imagine the bustle and excitement of early commerce on the Potomac River.

3 River Tours

Spirit Cruise Line: 1-866-404-8439, www.spiritcruises.com ▪ **Potomac Riverboat Company: 877-511-2628, www.potomacriverboatco.com**

Visitors can still use the Potomac River to reach Mount Vernon. Two tour boat lines serve the wharf from the city: Spirit Cruise Line and Potomac Riverboat Company. Spirit Cruise Line also offers summer river sightseeing tours originating and ending at Mount Vernon's wharf.

4 Slave Quarters

Many slaves had living spaces distributed across the plantation so that they were conveniently close to the work they were assigned. The remaining slaves lived communally in these quarters on the edge of the estate. In his will, Washington freed all his slaves and made provision for their ongoing support. Memorials to his slaves, erected in 1983, are located at the slave burial ground southwest of Washington's tomb, which itself is at the southwest end of the plantation.

5 Washington's Tomb

This tomb is the second to hold the remains of George and Martha Washington. It was erected in 1831 based on Washington's own instructions and, in the years since, the tomb has been visited by millions of people who come to pay their respects to the first US president.

6 Upper and Lower Gardens

The wonderfully colorful upper flower garden is densely planted with varieties known to be cultivated in Washington's time. The lower garden is surrounded by boxwood bushes that were planted before Washington's death. This orderly and expansive plot yielded a wealth of vegetables and berries for the plantation's kitchens.

7 The Greenhouse

The handsome greenhouse complex once helped protect exotic and valuable plants through the cold Virginian winter. Revolutionary-War-era visitors to Mount Vernon could enjoy English grapes, lemons, limes, and oranges, as well as a host of flowering tropical plants.

8 Museum

Over 700 artifacts offer an in-depth look at Washington's life and career from his early days as a surveyor to his post-presidency days at Mount Vernon. Among the items on display are his dress sword, his dentures, and his field bed from the Revolutionary War.

Gristmill and distillery

9 Gristmill and Distillery
Route 235 S ■ Open Apr–Oct: 10am–5pm daily

Located 3 miles (5 km) west of the estate is Washington's 18th-century watermill, which played an important part in his vision for America as a "granary to the world." Today, millers in colonial costume grind wheat into flour and corn into meal just as was done in the 1700s. Archaeologists excavated the site of Washington's 1797 whiskey distillery, and a fully reconstructed distillery now provides demonstrations and hands-on activities for visitors.

10 Pioneer Farm

George Washington was passionate about improving the agricultural methods of his time. The Pioneer Farm showcases many new ideas and techniques he worked with, including a redesigned plow, crop rotation, and even organic farming. But families will most enjoy meeting the animals of the colonial farm, including Ossabaur Island pigs, Hog Island sheep, and Devon cattle.

Greenhouse and garden

The Top 10 of Everything

The ornate Great Hall of the
Library of Congress

⏱🔟 Moments in History

Armies at the end of the Civil War on Pennsylvania Avenue in Washington, DC

1 Foundation of the Federal City

The US Constitution, ratified in 1788, provided and planned for "a District (not exceeding ten Miles square) as may, by Cession of Particular States..., become the Seat of the Government of the United States."

2 Layout and Design

In 1790, George Washington selected Pierre Charles L'Enfant, a French engineer, to lay out the city. The plan was influenced by Versailles and the city of Paris.

3 Expansion

Thomas Jefferson began western expansion by organizing the Lewis and Clark expedition in 1803. The C&O Canal, built between 1828 and 1850, and the Baltimore and Ohio Railroad, founded in 1828, provided a means of commerce through the mountains and launched a period of prosperity. New states were added to the Union, and bitter divisions arose connected to the issue of slavery.

4 War of 1812

The United States declared war on Britain in 1812, seeking freedom of marine trade and the security of US seamen. In 1814, British troops entered the capital and burned government buildings, including the White House and the Capitol. If it had not rained, the whole city might have burned down.

5 Civil War

Conflict between the Union and the seceding Southern states began on April 12, 1861, plunging Washington and the nation into crisis. Union supporters, joined by thousands of blacks escaping slavery in the South, doubled the city's population in four years. Although threatened, the city was never taken by Confederate troops and, when the war ended in 1865, Washington was unharmed.

The burning of the city in 1812

6 McMillan Plan

The McMillan Plan of 1901, so named for its congressional supporter, Senator James McMillan, was the first ever application of city planning in the US. It created much of the current layout of the Mall and President's Park.

7 New Deal

The Roosevelt era (1933–45) brought tremendous growth to the city. Efforts to bring the nation out of the Great Depression increased the size and number of government agencies, and provided direct funds for construction. Most of the buildings in the Federal Triangle, the completion of the Supreme Court, and the National Gallery of Art were New Deal works.

8 World War II

More than 10 percent of the US population of approximately 115 million was in uniform at the peak of the war, and the central management of all of these troops remained in Washington, DC.

Dr. Martin Luther King, Jr.

9 March on Washington

African-American leaders led 250,000 people to rally before the Lincoln Memorial on August 28, 1963 in support of equal rights. Dr. Martin Luther King, Jr.'s eloquent dream for America, along with the size of the march, gave impetus to the struggle.

10 Home Rule

The federal government's control over the city was modified with the Home Rule Charter in 1973. This legislation gave the city power to elect its own mayor and council.

TOP 10 CITIZEN RIGHTS OF THE CONSTITUTION

United States Constitution

1 Inherent Rights
Freedom of religion, speech, the press, assembly, and seeking redress of citizen grievances.

2 Legality of Arms
The right of the people to keep and bear arms.

3 Quartering of Soldiers
Freedom from housing soldiers in private homes in peacetime and in war, except as prescribed by law.

4 Unjustified Searches
Freedom from unreasonable search and seizure of people, houses, and effects without a warrant.

5 Limits on Prosecutors
A grand jury indictment is required before trial; a person cannot be tried more than once for the same crime; a person cannot be forced to testify against himself; a person's property cannot be confiscated without compensation.

6 Protection of the Accused
Accused persons will be given a trial by a jury of peers, be informed of the charges, be able to confront witnesses, and be represented by counsel.

7 Civil Case Jury Trial
In common law, parties have a right to a trial by jury.

8 Unjust Punishment
The government cannot require excessive bail, impose excessive fines, or use cruel or unusual punishment.

9 Limited Scope
The stated rights do not limit other rights.

10 State Powers
All powers not granted to the US government belong to the states.

TOP 10 US Presidents

George Washington

1 George Washington
The first president of the United States, Washington (1789–97), was never greater than when he refused to interpret the position of president as equivalent to "king."

2 John Adams
Adams (1797–1801) was among the young nation's most experienced diplomats, having managed affairs in Europe. He was the first US vice president, under Washington.

3 Thomas Jefferson
Jefferson (1801–9) is remembered for his embrace of democracy and his strong opposition to federal power.

4 James Madison
Madison (1809–17) demurred when he was called "the Father of the Constitution," stating that many minds had contributed, but there is little doubt that the Federalist Papers, which he co-authored, helped gain its ratification.

5 Andrew Jackson
The success of Jackson (1829–37) as a leader in the Battle of New Orleans in 1814–15 made him a national hero. His popularity helped him win battles with Congress and with private business interests over issues such as banking and tariffs.

6 Abraham Lincoln
Unquestionably one of the greatest ever political leaders in any nation, Lincoln (1861–5) overcame inexpressible odds in preserving the Union and beginning the process of freeing slaves.

7 Theodore Roosevelt
The dawning of the 20th century brought an energetic and activist president to the helm. Roosevelt (1901–9) became famous for his military exploits in the Spanish– American War, but is best known for his opposition to business monopolies and pursuing a strong foreign policy. He also established the National Parks system in the US.

8 Woodrow Wilson
Wilson (1913–21) was a quiet academic who faced the greatest foreign task the nation had ever seen – participation in World War I. Wilson successfully set into place a legislative program that controlled unfair business practices, reduced tariffs, forbade child labor, and improved the banking system. He was awarded the Nobel Peace Prize in 1919.

John Adams

9 Franklin D. Roosevelt

Roosevelt's (1933–45) efforts to overcome the Great Depression never succeeded in the broadest sense, but they inculcated the federal government with a sense of respect for the rights and needs of the common man and the poorest of the poor. He led valiantly during World War II.

Franklin D. Roosevelt

10 John F. Kennedy

Kennedy (1961–3) brought an unprecedented style and flair to the presidency and can be credited with possibly the most important action of the 20th century – the prevention of nuclear war over Soviet missiles placed in Cuba. His assassination cut short his pursuit of a plan for progressive social programs, including more freedom and justice for African-Americans.

John F. Kennedy

TOP 10 FIRST LADIES

Hillary Clinton

1 Martha Washington
Martha established the role of the First Lady imitated by her successors. She was famous for accompanying George on military campaigns.

2 Dolley Madison
Dolley's social appeal greatly helped her slightly awkward husband.

3 Sarah Polk
The wife of James K. Polk (1845–9) was a strong force in the administration, writing speeches for the president.

4 Mary Todd Lincoln
Mary staunchly supported Lincoln and the Union during the Civil War. Their son died three years before her husband's assassination in 1865.

5 Grace Coolidge
The wife of Calvin Coolidge (1923–9) had a charm and tact that made her one of America's best-loved women.

6 Eleanor Roosevelt
Eleanor's interests were equal rights and social justice. She greatly increased the diplomatic role of the First Lady.

7 Jacqueline Kennedy
A stylish socialite, Jackie was an instant hit with the public and visiting diplomats.

8 Lady Bird Johnson
Wife of Lyndon B. Johnson (1963–9), Lady Bird's beautification projects had a direct impact on DC.

9 Hillary Clinton
The former First Lady (1993–2001) has gone on to be a Senator (2001–9), Secretary of State (2009–13) and presidential candidate (2016).

10 Michelle Obama
A Harvard Law School graduate, she was a top lawyer, Chicago city administrator, and community outreach worker before becoming the 44th First Lady (2009–2017).

TOP10 Places of African-American History

1 Lincoln Memorial

This memorial touches the hearts of all African-Americans because of Abraham Lincoln's steadfastness in ending slavery in the US. It was here that Martin Luther King, Jr. made his "I Have a Dream" speech *(see p86)*.

Martin Luther King, Jr. Memorial

2 Martin Luther King, Jr. Memorial

MAP Q5 ■ 1964 Independence Ave, SW ■ Open 24 hours daily

The Mall's first monument to an African-American, the Martin Luther King memorial commemorates the work of the Baptist minister, civil rights activist, and inspirational orator. The two massive stone sculptures were designed by the Chinese sculptor Lei Yixin.

3 Metropolitan African Methodist Episcopal Church

MAP P3 ■ 1518 M St, NW

This church was important in sheltering runaway slaves before the Civil War, and its pulpit has hosted many respected speakers, including Frederick Douglass, Martin Luther King, Jr., and Jesse Jackson. The funeral of civil-rights activist Rosa Parks was held here in 2005.

4 Anacostia Community Museum

MAP E4 ■ 1901 Fort Place, SE ■ Open 10am–5pm daily

This museum explores the role that African-Americans have played in the culture of the nation as well as in contemporary urban communities.

5 Frederick Douglass National Historic Site

Frederick Douglass, a former slave, made many speeches for the rights of African-Americans, and was an adviser to Abraham Lincoln. He and his wife, Anna, moved into this Gothic-Italian-style house in 1877 *(see p49)*. In the garden is a humble stone hut nicknamed "The Growlery," which Douglass used as a study.

6 Mary McLeod Bethune Council House

A former cotton-picker, Bethune rose to be a leading educator of African-Americans and an activist for equal rights. Her home was headquarters of the National Council of Negro Women. She was also an adviser to Franklin D. Roosevelt *(see p49)*.

Mary McLeod Bethune Council House

7 Mount Zion United Methodist Church

MAP L2 ■ 1334 29th St, NW ■ 202-234-0148 ■ Services Sun 10:45am; open by appt at other times

Founded in 1816, this was believed to be the first black congregation in the District. The original building was an important stop on the Underground Railroad. The present red-brick church was built in 1884. A small cottage holds artifacts reflecting the black history of Georgetown.

8 Lincoln Park

Lincoln Park statue

This pleasant park does justice to its dedication to Lincoln. The 1974 Robert Berks statue of Mary McLeod Bethune shows the great educator passing the tools of culture on to younger generations. The Emancipation Statue by Thomas Ball (1876) shows Lincoln holding his Proclamation in the presence of a slave escaping his chains (see p82).

9 African American Civil War Memorial and Museum

MAP Q1 ■ 1925 Vermont Ave, NW ■ 202-667-2667 ■ Open 10am–6pm Mon–Fri, 10am–4pm Sat, noon–4pm Sun ■ www.afroamcivilwar.org

This small museum uses artifacts, photographs, and exhibits to highlight the contributions of the more than 200,000 African-Americans who fought in the Civil War.

10 National Museum of African American History and Culture

This striking new museum has a collection of artifacts documenting and highlighting the lives, history, and culture of African-Americans. Due to the museum's popularity, passes are required for timed entry (see p55).

TOP 10 AFRICAN-AMERICAN FIGURES

The singer Marian Anderson

1 Ralph Bunche
The first African-American to receive the Nobel Peace Prize, because of his diplomatic efforts in the UN.

2 Duke Ellington
The musical genius was a native of Washington. He played his first paid performance on U Street.

3 Dr. Martin Luther King, Jr.
The charismatic leader of the civil rights movement.

4 Paul Lawrence Dunbar
Dunbar rose from poverty to gain recognition as a poet – the first African-American to do so – publishing his first collection in 1892.

5 Harriet Tubman
The best-known figure who freed slaves through the secret Underground Railroad network in the 19th century.

6 Ida B. Wells-Barnett
This celebrated crusader against anti-black government actions also joined the 1913 women's suffrage rally.

7 Marian Anderson
In 1939, the singer was barred from Constitution Hall because of her race, so gave her Easter Sunday concert at the Lincoln Memorial instead.

8 Eleanor Holmes Norton
Norton has been effective as a non-voting House member, lobbying to promote Washington issues.

9 Walter E. Washington
Mayor of Washington from 1975 to 1979, the first elected mayor in the city for over 100 years.

10 Barack Obama
In 2008, Obama was elected as the US's first African-American president and served from 2009 to 2017.

Historic Homes and Buildings

1 Carnegie Library
MAP Q3 ■ Mt Vernon Sq, NW

Philanthropist Andrew Carnegie campaigned to build libraries across America and funded 1,679 in all. This magnificent Beaux Arts building has been restored and is occupied by the Historical Society of Washington, DC.

2 Decatur House
MAP N3 ■ 1610 H Street, NW ■ 202-218-4338 ■ Open 11am–2pm Mon ■ Tours 11am, 12:30pm & 2pm Mon

Stephen Decatur, a renowned naval hero, built this Federal-style town-house in 1818. It now houses the White House Historical Association, but has been preserved to evoke 19th-century middle-class America.

3 Gadsby's Tavern Museum
MAP D5 ■ 134 N Royal St, Alexandria, VA ■ 703-746-4242 ■ Open Apr–Oct: 10am–5pm Tue–Sat, 1–5pm Sun–Mon; Nov–Mar: 11am–4pm Wed–Sat, 1–4pm Sun ■ Adm

Two buildings occupy this site: the 1792 City Hotel, and the 1785 tavern where early American leaders, including Washington and Jefferson, dined. Today this National Historic Landmark houses a city museum and a fine-dining restaurant.

Ford's Theatre facade

4 Ford's Theatre

The theater where Lincoln was shot in 1865 by John Wilkes Booth has been restored by the federal government. It is now a memorial to the music- and theater-loving president. There is a museum on site and the building also hosts theater productions (see p95).

5 Woodrow Wilson House
MAP M1 ■ 2340 S St, NW ■ 202-387-4062 ■ Open 10am–4pm Wed–Sun (Jan–Feb: Fri–Sun) ■ Adm

President Woodrow Wilson moved into this Georgian Revival house in 1921 after serving as the 28th president of the United States. The marble entry, staircase, and solarium are highlights and the Wilson furnishings are from 1924.

The drawing room of Woodrow Wilson House

(6) Frederick Douglass National Historic Site

MAP E4 ■ 1411 W St, SE ■ 202-426-5961 ■ Open Apr–Oct: 9am–5pm daily (until 4:30pm Nov–Mar); closed Thanksgiving, Dec 25, Jan 1 ■ www.nps.gov/frdo

Frederick Douglass and his wife Anna were the very first African American family in Anacostia when they moved to this house in 1877. Born a slave, Douglass became America's most effective anti-slavery speaker and writer (see p46).

(7) Mary McLeod Bethune Council House

MAP P2 ■ 1318 Vermont Ave, NW ■ 202-673-2402 ■ Open 9am–5pm daily

The renowned teacher (see p46) and advocate for women's and African-American rights bought this Victorian townhouse – now a National Historic Site – in 1935. It is still furnished with her possessions.

Dumbarton Oaks

(8) Dumbarton Oaks

This remarkable Federal-style home (1801) is filled with a Harvard-curated collection of Byzantine and pre-Columbian art. The house is surrounded by lovely gardens, with an orangery whose walls are draped in a 150-year-old ficus (see p105).

(9) Old Stone House

The oldest surviving structure in DC, this evocative building holds demonstrations of crafts and skills of pre-Revolutionary life (see p107).

(10) Belmont-Paul House

Built in 1800, this enchanting home is one of the oldest on Capitol Hill. It is now a museum of women's emancipation (see p80).

TOP 10 ARCHITECTURAL SIGHTS

National Building Museum

1 National Building Museum
Displays examine architecture, design, engineering, and city planning (see p95).

2 Eisenhower Executive Office Building
MAP N4 ■ 1650 Pennsylvania Ave, NW ■ www.whitehouse.gov
The extravagant decoration is a favorite with architecture buffs.

3 Treasury Building
This 1836 Greek Revival building retains original features (see p100).

4 The Octagon
This building is now a museum of architecture and design (see p100).

5 Library of Congress
This extensive library contains more than 38 million books (see p79).

6 Old Post Office Pavilion
MAP P4 ■ 1100 Pennsylvania Ave, NW ■ www.nps.gov/opot
This iconic Romanesque revival building was completed in 1899.

7 Pope-Leighey House
Alexandria, VA ■ US 1 and Rte 235 ■ Open Apr–Dec: 11am–4pm Fri–Mon ■ Adm
The city's most innovative Frank Lloyd Wright design.

8 Supreme Court Building
This marble edifice never fails to delight (see p80).

9 Anderson House
MAP M2 ■ 2118 Massachusetts Ave, NW ■ Open 1–4pm Tue–Sat, noon–4pm Sun
This Beaux Arts mansion was built in 1905 for Ambassador Lars Anderson.

10 Cox's Row
MAP K2 ■ 3327–29 N St, NW
These Federal-style townhouses are outstanding examples of domestic architecture of the early 19th century.

🔟 Memorials and Monuments

The Franklin D. Roosevelt Memorial depicting the president and his dog

1 Lincoln Memorial

The majestic monument to the president who preserved America's unity and began the process of ending slavery is built in the form of a Greek temple. Daniel Chester French designed the enormous statue of a seated Abraham Lincoln in 1915, and it is among America's most inspiring sites, especially for its association with the African-American struggle for equality and opportunity *(see p86)*.

2 Washington Monument

This spire is the dominant feature on the city skyline, 555 ft (170 m) high and clad in gleaming white marble. One of the tallest freestanding masonry constructions in the world, built between 1848 and 1884, the obelisk can be seen for miles *(see p87)*.

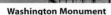

Washington Monument

3 Franklin D. Roosevelt Memorial

This popular memorial, dedicated by President Clinton in 1997, has four outdoor "rooms," representing Roosevelt's four terms as president. Each is a composition of statues, water, plantings, and engraved quotations. He is accompanied here, as in life, by his beloved Scottish terrier Fala, who rarely left his side. The memorial is a focus for activists for disabled citizens – Roosevelt was partially paralyzed by polio *(see p88)*.

4 Jefferson Memorial

One of Jefferson's favorite Classical designs, the Pantheon in Rome, inspired this graceful monument. Dedicated in 1943 on the 200th anniversary of his birth, it houses a 19-ft (6-m) bronze statue of him by Rudolph Evans. The temple is especially enchanting when floodlit at night *(see p88)*.

5 Vietnam Veterans Memorial

This simple V-shaped black granite wall features the names of all those who died in this divisive war. The 1982 memorial is the work of Maya Lin, at the time a 21-year-old architecture student at Yale *(see p86)*.

6 Korean War Veterans Memorial

Nineteen steel statues dominate in this memorial to the Americans who died in the UN's "police action" in Korea. A wall is etched with faces of actual soldiers. A circular pool invites quiet reflection (see p88).

7 The Pentagon

MAP C4 ■ 2024 Pentagon Pedestrian Tunnel, Arlington, VA ■ pentagontours.osd.mil/Tours

With well over 17 miles (27 km) of corridors, the US military headquarters is the world's largest office. The 60-minute free tour covers 1.5 miles (2.5 km) of the complex and includes military history, the 9/11 Memorial, and the Hall of Heroes. Visitors need to book 14 days in advance.

8 World War II Memorial

This memorial honors the 16 million who served in the US military during World War II, as well as the civilians who helped (see p88).

9 African-American Civil War Memorial

MAP P1 ■ 1000 U St, NW

"The Spirit of Freedom," a 1996 sculpture by Ed Hamilton, depicts African-American Union soldiers facing the enemy.

10 Iwo Jima Statue (Marine Corps Memorial)

MAP K5 ■ 1400 N Meade St, Arlington, VA

Marines struggling to erect the Stars and Stripes on a ridge at Iwo Jima serves as a memorial to all marines who have fought for their country. The Pacific island saw fierce fighting, resulting in 7,000 American deaths, during World War II.

Iwo Jima Statue

TOP 10 STATUES

Abraham Lincoln Memorial

1 Abraham Lincoln
The marble vision of the president dominates the memorial (see p96).

2 Neptune Fountain
Roland Hinton Perry created this grouping at the Library of Congress between 1897 and 1898 (see p79).

3 Albert Einstein
MAP M4 ■ 2101 Constitution Ave, NW
This 1979 bronze by Robert Berks shows the great thinker in front of the National Academy of Sciences.

4 Benjamin Franklin
MAP P4 ■ 1100 Pennsylvania Ave, NW
Jacques Jouvenal's statue at the Old Post Office honors Franklin's creation of the US Postal Service.

5 First Division Monument
MAP N4 ■ State Place & 17th St, NW
A shining tribute to the First Infantry Division of World War I.

6 Andrew Jackson
MAP N3 ■ Lafayette Sq, NW
This heroic equestrian statue was created by Clark Mills in 1853.

7 Winston Churchill
MAP H5 ■ Massachusetts Ave, NW
A 1966 sculpture by William M. McVey symbolizes the friendship between Britain and the US.

8 Ulysses S. Grant Memorial
This grouping took Henry Merwin Shrady 20 years to complete (see p82).

9 Theodore Roosevelt
MAP L4 ■ Roosevelt Island
Paul Manship's bronze work shows the president gesticulating to his listeners.

10 Joan of Arc
MAP P1 ■ Meridian Hill Park, Florida Ave & 16th St, NW
This 1922 work was a gift from the women of France to those of the US.

×REVOLUTIONARY·WAR·1775–1783× FRENC

🔟 Museums

A Douglas DC-3 aircraft on display at the National Air and Space Museum

① National Air and Space Museum

The 20th century's love affair with flight, from its intrepid beginnings to the mastery of space travel, is explored here *(see pp20–21)*.

② National Museum of the American Indian

The Smithsonian's huge collection of material and artifacts related to Native American art, history, culture, and language moved into its first permanent home in 2004. Items include North American carvings, quilled hides, feathered bonnets, pottery, and contemporary art, plus Mexican, Caribbean, and Central and South American objects *(see p85)*.

③ National Museum of Natural History

Must-see exhibits abound: the Hall of Human Origins depicting human evolution over six million years; the Live Insect Zoo; the Don Pedro aquamarine and Hope diamond in the National Gem collection; and a stunning mammal exhibit *(see pp28–9)*.

④ National Museum of American History

Combining the "America's Attic" approach with fine contemporary interpretive exhibits, the museum offers visitors a fascinating look into America's past *(see pp22–3)*.

⑤ United States Holocaust Memorial Museum

Designed by James Ingo Freed and referencing Holocaust sites via its abstract architectural forms, this museum traces the Holocaust in Europe, grimly detailing the surveillance and the loss of individual rights faced by Jews, political objectors, gypsies, homosexuals, and the

Interior of the National Museum of the American Indian

Previous pages Iwo Jima Statue (Marine Corps Memorial) at sunset handicapped. Moving eyewitness accounts, photographs, and artifacts all help to tell the story (see pp86–7).

6 National Postal Museum
Mail and fun don't naturally go together, but at this wonderfully conceived museum, they do. The little Pony Express carriage, tunnel-like construction representing the desolate roads faced by the earliest mail carriers, and the mail-sorting railroad car all entertain and inform visitors (see p81).

7 International Spy Museum
This fascinating museum explores the role that spies have played in events throughout history. The exhibitions display equipment, tell the stories of individuals, and reveal their missions and techniques (see p96).

8 National Archives of the United States
The Rotunda of the National Archives displays the foundation documents of America: the Constitution of the United States, the Declaration of Independence, and the Bill of Rights. There are exciting interactive activities in the Public Vaults (see p88).

9 Newseum
This unique museum recounts the history of news gathering and the evolution of electronic communication.

Significant moments in history such as the fall of the Berlin Wall and the 9/11 terrorist attacks have their own galleries (see p95).

National Museum of African American History and Culture

10 National Museum of African American History and Culture
MAP P4 ■ 1400 Constitution Ave, NW ■ 202-633-1000 ■ Open 10am–5:30pm daily; closed Dec 25 ■ ■ Entry by free timed passes ■ www.nmaahc.si.edu

Opened in 2016, this excellent museum is set in a striking bronze-clad contemporary building on the National Mall. It contains over 35,000 artifacts, including an early 1800's slave cabin, a shawl given to 19th-century abolitionist Harriet Tubman (see p47) by Queen Victoria, and Chuck Berry's red Cadillac.

⏏10 Art Galleries

Degas' *Dancers at the Barre*

1 The Phillips Collection
MAP M2 ▪ 1600 21st St, NW ▪ 202-387-2151 ▪ Open 10am–5pm Tue–Sat (to 8:30pm Thu); noon–6:30pm Sun ▪ Adm

Established in 1921, the Phillips Collection is America's first museum of modern art. It is celebrated for its Impressionist works, including Renoir's *Luncheon of the Boating Party*, Pierre Bonnard's *Open Window*, and Degas' *Dancers at the Barre*.

2 National Gallery of Art
Displaying one of the most distinguished art collections in the world, Washington's magnificent National Gallery of Art gives its visitors a broad but in-depth look at the development of American and European art from the Middle Ages to the 20th century *(see pp24–7)*.

3 National Portrait Gallery
Portraits of remarkable Americans who shaped the country are on display at this gallery. Its highlights include a complete collection of portraits of all the presidents of America, and American Origins, a chronologically arranged exhibit showcasing encounters between Native Americans and European explorers from the early years into the early 20th century *(see p96)*.

4 Renwick Gallery
This gallery is considered by many Washingtonians as their favorite, not least because it is housed in a gorgeous French Renaissance-style building, as well as staging well-organized shows of American crafts. The Grand Salon, previously styled as a 19th-century picture gallery, was the subject of an international design competition to "re-envision" it as a contemporary exhibition space *(see p99)*.

5 Hirshhorn Museum and Sculpture Garden
The Hirshhorn exhibits the most varied modern and contemporary art in Washington, DC. The collection of 12,000 artworks by leading artists, from the late 19th century to the present, includes paintings, sculptures, and mixed media, as well as photographs, works on paper, and new media. Exhibitions change frequently, displaying art by emerging or well-known artists, illustrating a major trend, or highlighting historical developments *(see p85)*.

Hirshhorn Museum and Sculpture Garden

⑥ Freer Gallery of Art

MAP P5 ■ Jefferson Drive at 12th St, SW ■ 202-633-1000 ■ Opening times vary, check website ■ www.asia.si.edu

Following extensive renovations, the intimate and tranquil Freer Gallery reopened in 2017. The elegant exhibit spaces, with Terrazzo floors, have returned to their original 1923 splendor. Its collection spans 6,000 years with more than 22,000 works. The permanent exhibitions feature art from he Middle East, East Asia, and the Indian subcontinent, while the temporary exhibitions highlight the many cultures represented here.

⑦ Arthur M. Sackler Gallery

MAP Q5 ■ 1050 Independence Ave, SW ■ 202-633-1000 ■ Open 10am–5:30pm daily; closed Dec 25 ■ www.asia.si.edu

Another of the underground museums of the Smithsonian, the Sackler is a leading center for the study and display of ancient and contemporary Asian art. Its events bring Asian art and philosophies to life, and its occasional presentations of Tibetan monks carrying out the ritual of sand-painting a mandala are always huge hits.

Bronze Shiva, Arthur M. Sackler Gallery

⑧ National Museum of African Art

This harmonious building brings architectural features common in Africa to one of the Smithsonian's most innovative museums, built principally underground. The wonderful permanent collection provides the best introduction to the role of art in African culture that one could hope to find (see p88). The pieces on display include ceramics, musical instruments, textiles, tools, masks, and figurines.

⑨ National Museum of Women in the Arts

This is the only museum in the world dedicated exclusively to displaying the work of women artists, from the Renaissance to the present day. Fascinating and provocative exhibitions explore the work and social role of female artists over the centuries, as well as that of women in general (see p96).

⑩ Kreeger Museum

MAP G5 ■ 2401 Foxhall Rd, NW ■ 202-337-3050 ■ Open 10am–4pm Tue–Sat ■ Tours 10:30am and 1:30pm Tue–Fri, 10:30am, noon, and 1:30pm Sat ■ Adm

This relatively unknown private museum houses Impressionist works by 19th- and 20th-century painters and sculptors such as Rodin, Kandinsky, and Monet, works by Washington artists, and traditional works of art from Africa and Asia.

TOP 10 Off the Beaten Path

George Mason Memorial

1 George Mason Memorial
MAP N6 ■ www.nps.gov/gemm

Sometimes called the "forgotten Founding Father," George Mason was instrumental in framing the US Constitution and creating the Bill of Rights. Located near the Jefferson Memorial, the Mason Memorial is an open plaza with flower gardens and a fountain. A statue of a smiling, seated Mason is popular with children, who climb into his lap to have their picture taken.

2 Kenilworth Aquatic Gardens

Laid out in 1882, these gardens feature numerous ponds filled with lotus and water lilies that bloom from May to July. A trail through the surrounding Anacostia River marshlands makes this a fascinating stop for nature- and bird-lovers (see p61).

3 The Old Stone House

This charming blue granite Georgetown house dates from 1765, making it the oldest building in the Washington, DC area. In constant use as a shop or home until its purchase by the government in 1953, it offers a fascinating look at what 18th-century life was like (see p107). Behind the vernacular house is an inviting Colonial Revival garden.

4 Lock-keeper's House
MAP N4 ■ Corner of 17th Street and Constitution Ave, NW ■ Not open to the public

This small stone building offers a unique insight into DC's colorful past. In the 1800s, a branch of the C&O Canal ran where the avenue is today, and it was the keeper's job to operate the locks, raising and lowering passing barges, and to collect toll.

5 National Postal Museum

This museum should be high on any visitor's list for the sheer fun it has relating the story of the American postal service. Historic biplanes hang from the high ceiling, while a real stagecoach is frozen in time, rushing mail to the wild west. Other exhibits include rare and unusual stamps, artifacts from the Pony Express, and even mail carried by Amelia Earhart on her famous transatlantic flight (see p81).

National Postal Museum

6 National Museum of Health and Medicine
MAP C2 ■ 2500 Linden Lane, Silver Spring, MD 20910 ■ 301-319-3300 ■ Open 10am–5:30pm daily ■ www.medicalmuseum.mil

Established by the US Army in 1862 to collect and study specimens for the advancement of Army medicine and surgery, this unique collection holds over 25 million fascinating (if somewhat morbid and not for everyone) items, including photos, historic medical artifacts, and preserved human remains. Exhibits include Civil War-era bones and skulls showing battle wounds, and the bullet that killed President Abraham Lincoln in 1865.

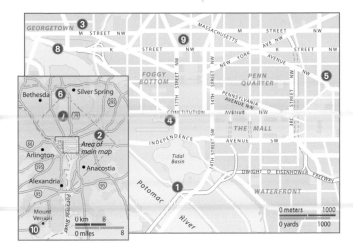

7 Peirce Mill
MAP J4 ■ Tilden Street, NW
■ Open Jan & Feb: noon–4pm Sat &
Sun; Mar: 10am–4pm Sat & Sun; Apr–
Oct: 10am–4pm Wed–Sun; Nov & Dec:
10am–4pm Sat & Sun ■ 202-895-6070
■ www.nps.gov/pimi

This historic grist mill in Rock Creek
Park (see pp60–61) was built in the
1820s and restored in the early
2000s. A tour of the mill offers a
glimpse into DC's past, and you can
enjoy a hike or picnic by sparkling
Rock Creek. Demonstrations of the
mill grinding grain are held from
April to October, 11am to 2pm every
second and fourth Saturday.

8 Georgetown Waterfront Park
MAP L3

This pretty, tree-shaded park offers
fine views of the busy Potomac from
Lincoln Center to old Georgetown.
Benches and a waterfront walkway
make it a good place for relaxing,
strolling, and picnicking.

9 National Geographic Museum

Anyone who has been thrilled by
National Geographic magazine or TV
documentaries will enjoy this small
museum that showcases the famous
photography of the magazine as well
as constantly changing exhibits that
highlight current stories and the
work of the Society. Oddities abound,
such as the 3D model of the Grand
Canyon on the ceiling (see p101).

10 George Washington's Distillery
5513 Mount Vernon Memorial Hwy
Alexandria, VA 22309 ■ Open Apr–Oct:
10am–5pm daily; Nov–Mar: 9am–
4pm daily ■ www.mountvernon.org

Washington's most successful
business venture was making
whiskey. His distillery and grist mill,
located about 3 miles (5 km) from
the Mount Vernon estate, operate
using methods and equipment
typical of Washington's era. Entrance
to the site is available only with a
ticket to Mount Vernon (see pp36–9).

George Washington's Distillery

🔟 Green Spaces

The Smithsonian Castle presides over the Enid A. Haupt Garden

1 Enid A. Haupt Garden

These gardens sit on top of the Smithsonian Museums, and are inspired by the culture on display below. The Moongate Garden beside the Sackler Gallery reflects the Asian world, with its circular pool, pink granite, and cherry and beech trees. The Fountain Garden, alongside the Museum of African Art, evokes a Moorish ambience, with cascading waters and shaded seats (see p88).

2 US Botanic Garden

The gleaming glass-walled conservatory building is a beautiful home for this "living plant museum." Microclimates, such as desert, tropics, and Mediterranean, reveal the variety and beauty of plant adaptations. Don't miss the primitive ferns dating back 150 million years.

US Botanic Garden

Outside is the variegated National Garden with an environmental learning center (see p80).

3 Chesapeake and Ohio Canal

Boats on this 184-mile (295-km) 19th-century waterway carried cargo between Maryland and Georgetown for 100 years before the railroad put it out of business. It is now a National Historical Park, a haven for walkers and cyclists. Interpreted canal boat tours will resume in 2019 (see p105).

4 National Arboretum

MAP E3 ▪ 3501 New York Ave, NE ▪ Open 8am–5pm daily; closed Dec 31 ▪ www.usna.usda.gov

An acclaimed bonsai display – some trees are almost 400 years old – is one of the many collections that flourish on these 446 acres (180 ha). Azaleas, dogwoods, magnolias, box-woods, and roses abound. A stand of columns, formerly on the US Capitol, adds a classical air (see p71).

5 Rock Creek Park

MAP J1 ▪ 5200 Glover Rd, NW ▪ Open dawn–dusk daily, check website for details ▪ www.nps.gov/rocr

This vast National Park meanders with its namesake creek, offering something for everyone: there are lovely woodland trails and nature

Cherry trees at Dumbarton Oaks

programs, bicycle paths, tennis courts, a golf course, playing fields, and picnic areas.

6 Dumbarton Oaks

Magnificent trees, including ancient oaks, soar above the park and gardens surrounding this historic Federal-style house. Designed by Beatrix Jones Farrand, the gardens range from formal to more casual settings. In spring, they are a mass of cherry blossom, and from March to October they are ablaze with wisteria, roses, lilies, and perennial borders. Pools and fountains tie the ensemble together (see p105).

7 Theodore Roosevelt Island

MAP L4 ■ George Washington Memorial Parkway ■ Open 6am–10pm daily

This wooded island on the Potomac River is the perfect memorial to the president who valued conservation. A 17-ft (5-m) statue of Roosevelt is the centerpiece of what is otherwise a monument to nature – an unspoiled, idyllic space for bird-watching, hiking, fishing, and relaxing.

8 Bartholdi Park and Fountain

The French sculptor of the Statue of Liberty, Frédéric Auguste Bartholdi (1834–1904), also created this reflection of *belle époque*

Theodore Roosevelt statue

majesty. The 30-ft (9-m) sculpture's three caryatids support a circular basin surmounted by three tritons. A small garden surrounds the fountain like the setting for a gemstone (see p80).

9 East Potomac Park

MAP P6 ■ 14th St, SW

One of Washington's best-kept secrets, this 300-acre (120-ha) peninsula has the Potomac River on one side and the boat-filled Washington Channel on the other. A paved walkway traces the waterfront, offering lovely views to runners, walkers, skaters, and fishermen. There is also a 9- and an 18-hole public golf course, and in spring thousands of cherry trees burst into lovely pink blossom.

East Potomac Park

10 Kenilworth Park and Aquatic Gardens

MAP E3 ■ Aquatic Gardens: 1550 Anacostia Ave, NE; open Apr–Oct: 9am–5pm daily, Nov–Mar: 8am–4pm daily; closed Jan 1, Thanksgiving Day, Dec 25 ■ Park: Kenilworth & Burroughs Aves; open 8am–dusk daily ■ www.nps.gov/keaq

The lovely 14-acre (6-ha) Aquatic Gardens began as a hobby for Civil War veteran Walter Benjamin Shaw in 1882. He later transformed it into a commercial water garden. Now run by the National Park Service, the gardens are known for the 20 or so ponds that are planted with water lilies and lotuses. The numerous varieties of local wildlife include birds, frogs, turtles, and butterflies. Adjacent Kenilworth Park offers acres of recreational areas and meadows.

Outdoor Activities

1 Running
Runners are seen everywhere in Washington. The Mall is popular, as are the walkways around the Tidal Basin, Georgetown Waterfront, the C&O Canal (see p60), East Potomac Park (see p61), and Rock Creek Park (see pp60–61).

2 In-Line Skating
Rock Creek Park (see pp60–61) has been named one of the top 10 sites in the nation for in-line skating, but most bike trails allow skaters as well. Rent skates and protective gear from the numerous in-line skating companies in the area.

3 Boating
Thompson Boat Center: MAP L3; 2900 Virginia Ave, NW; 202-333-9543; open Mar–Oct: hours vary, check website; www.thompsonboatcenter.com ■ **Washington Sailing Marina: MAP D5; 1 Marina Drive, Dangerfield Island, Alexandria, VA; 703-548-9027; open May–Nov: hours vary, check website; www.washingtonsailingmarina.com**

Georgetown's Thompson Boat Center rents kayaks, rowing shells, canoes, and sailboats to reach Roosevelt Island and tour the

waterfront. The Washington Sailing Marina rents sailboats for excursions on the Potomac. Make sure to call in advance about certification requirements.

4 Cycling
Bike and Roll: MAP Q4; 901 G St, NW; 202-842-2453; www.bikeandrolldc.com ■ **Capital Bikeshare: www.capitalbikeshare.com**

Both the Thompson Boat Center and the Washington Sailing Marina rent bicycles, and Capital Bikeshare has 440 stations in the area where you may use a credit card

Cycling by the US Capitol

to rent a bike for 30 minutes, a day, or three days. Favorite routes are the C&O Canal towpath (see p60) and the Mount Vernon Trail (see pp36–9). Bike and Roll offers tours and rentals.

5 Golf
East Potomac Park: MAP P6; 972 Ohio Drive, SW (Hain's Point); 202-554-7660 ■ **Rock Creek Park Golf Course: MAP D4; 6100 16th St, NW; 202-882-7332** ■ **Langston Golf Course: MAP E3; 2600 Benning Rd, NE; 202-397-8638**

There are over 100 golf courses in the vicinity. Public courses include East Potomac Park and the Rock Creek Park Golf Course. Langston

Sailboats at Washington Harbour

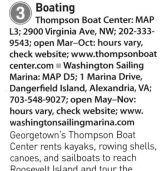

Golf Course, a few minutes from Capitol Hill, was among the first African-American courses in the US.

6 Hiking
Trails.com: www.trails.com

The 4-mile (7-km) Western Ridge Trail and 5-mile (8-km) Valley Trail, both in Rock Creek Park *(see pp60–61)*, are scenic and gentle. The 11.5-mile (18.5-km) Capital Crescent Trail follows the old B&O Railroad route through Georgetown north to Bethesda. Trail information available at Trails.com.

7 Informal Team Sports

Volleyball, dodgeball, rugby, softball, kickball, team Frisbee, and even polo are played on various fields at the western end of the Mall.

Kickball teams at play

8 Tennis
East Potomac Park Tennis Center: MAP P6; 1090 Ohio Drive, SW; 202-554-5962

The East Potomac Park Tennis Center is operated by the National Park Service. Indoor and outdoor courts are available.

9 Horseback Riding
Rock Creek Horse Center: MAP J2; 5100 Glover Rd, NW; 202-362-0117; open 10am–6pm Mon–Fri, 9am–5pm Sat & Sun

The Rock Creek Park Horse Center provides scheduled trail rides and riding lessons for all levels.

10 Climbing
Earth Treks: 725 Rockville Pike, Rockville, MD; 240-283-9942 ■ www.earthtreksclimbing.com/rockville

The city of Rockville has a climbing gym suited to all ages and abilities.

TOP 10 SPECTATOR SPORTS

Washington Redskins

1 Washington Redskins
The National Football League Redskins are a year-round local obsession. Games are at FedEx Field in Maryland. Tickets at www.ticketmaster.com

2 Washington Wizards
The National Basketball Association team plays at the Capital One Arena *(see p95)*. Buy tickets at the box office.

3 Washington Capitals
The National Hockey League team plays its home games at the Capital One Arena.

4 DC United
Audi Field at Buzzard Point, SW ■ 202-587-5000
Audi Field is home to professional soccer.

5 Baseball
Major league baseball team the Washington Nationals play at Nationals Park in DC, while the Baltimore Orioles play at Camden Yards in Baltimore.

6 Washington Mystics
The women's professional basketball team plays home games at the Capital One Arena.

7 Citi Open
www.citiopentennis.com
This mid-summer tournament attracts major tennis pros.

8 Georgetown University Basketball
College Park, MD ■ 202-397-SEAT
Fast-paced action at the Capital One Arena.

9 University of Maryland Athletics
ACC football and national basketball teams lead a varied program.

10 Naval Academy Football
The spectacle at these games is unmatched. Schedule and tickets: www.navysports.com

TOP 10 Children's Attractions

National Zoological Park

1 National Zoological Park

The animals in the city's zoo are housed in large, re-created natural habitats. Sea lion demonstrations are a delight. The Speedwell Conservation Carousel showcases endangered species under a colorful open-air pavilion (see pp32–3).

2 Six Flags America and Hurricane Harbor

13710 Central Avenue, Upper Marlboro, MD 20721 ■ Open Six Flags: Jun–Aug: 10:30am–6–9pm (hours vary) daily, Sep–May: days and hours vary; Hurricane Harbor: Jun–Sep: 11am–7pm daily (May: days and hours vary) ■ Adm ■ www.sixflags.com/america

Children ready for a break from the memorials and monuments will love these parks. Six Flags features ten massive roller coasters with names like Ragin' Cajun and Mind Eraser, along with plenty of rides for smaller kids. It is divided into several areas, including Mardi Gras, Coyote Creek, and the Batman-themed Gotham City. Younger children will adore Looney Tunes Movie Town. Hurricane Harbor is a huge water park with a dozen water slides and a massive wave pool.

3 National Air and Space Museum

Kids will be inspired by spectacular rockets and the 3D IMAX Journey Into Space, while their parents and grandparents can reminisce over the early days of aviation and space flight (see pp20–21).

4 The Capital Wheel at National Harbor

MAP D6 ■ 116 Waterfront St, MD 20745 ■ Open noon–10pm Mon–Thu, 10am–11pm Fri–Sun ■ Adm

The Capital Wheel at National Harbor lifts visitors 180 ft (55 m) above the ground in climate-controlled gondolas, offering fine views up and down the Potomac River from the National Mall to Mount Vernon.

5 Oxon Hill Farm

MAP D5 ■ 6411 Oxon Hill Rd, MD 20745 ■ Open 8am–4:30pm daily; closed Jan 1, Thanksgiving Day, Dec 25

Just a few miles from downtown DC, this working museum is a good place for kids to learn what rural farm life was like in the early 20th century. Children can join in with feeding the chickens, milking the cows, and riding on a hay wagon.

Six Flags America roller coaster

6 Wolftrap Children's Theater in the Woods

1551 Trap Road, Vienna, VA 22182 ■ Open late Jun–mid-Aug, see website for times ■ Adm ■ www.wolftrap.org

This endearing venue offers dance, music, puppetry, and plays for kids age 4 and up. The stage is down a pretty path in a woodland clearing. Most of the programs are interactive, encouraging kids to sing, dance, and get on stage with the performers.

7 Smithsonian Carousel

MAP P5 ■ **900 Jefferson Drive, SW** ■ Open 10am–5pm daily, weather permitting, closed Dec 23 ■ Adm

In front of the Arts and Industries Building at the Smithsonian is a delightful, authentic carousel with brightly painted hand-carved animals. It only runs in good weather, but don't miss this bit of old-world fun if you have the chance. It also makes a refreshing break for kids starting to tire of the museums.

Smithsonian Carousel

8 International Spy Museum

From a spy letter penned by George Washington to James Bond's Aston Martin, this unique museum offers a kid-pleasing glimpse into the world of spies and espionage. The museum's thousands of artifacts include gadgets such as a German World War II Enigma machine, an umbrella that fires poison pellets, and a KGB lipstick gun. Interactive activities allow kids to adopt disguises and undertake guided espionage activities. The Spy in the City Tour takes participants (10 and older) outside the museum, using a communications GPS to lead them through a simulated spy mission on the streets of DC (see p96).

9 National Museum of American History

This kid-friendly museum has some great hands-on action for its younger

National Museum of American History

visitors, including the Spark Lab with interactive exhibits exploring the process of invention. Activities are targeted at children aged 6 to 12, but there are also Object Project and Wegmans Wonderplace for younger kids; activities here explore the inter-relationship of innovative objects, people, and social change. America on the Move and the Star-Spangled Banner are also popular (see pp22–3).

10 National Museum of Natural History

There is plenty here to interest young visitors, in particular the Live Insect Zoo featuring live specimens of giant hissing cockroaches and large leaf-cutter ants, and the Dinosaur Hall (closed until 2019) which contains a cast of a nest of dinosaur eggs and reconstructions of dinosaur skel-etons. Q?rius encourages teens, tweens, and children (and adults) to hold and interact with objects such as crocodile heads and elephant tusks. The Live Butterfly Pavilion is home to exquisite species from around the world (see pp28–9).

National Museum of Natural History

🔟 Theaters

The multitiered auditorium of the historic Ford's Theatre

① Ford's Theatre

The tragedy of Abraham Lincoln's assassination here in 1865 kept this theater closed for over 100 years, but now it is the home of a vibrant theater company as well as being a museum, center for learning, and historic landmark *(see p95)*.

② Arena Stage
MAP Q6 ▪ 1101 6th St, SW
▪ 202-488-3300

Internationally renowned as a pioneering non-profit theater for over six decades, Arena has produced plenty of high-quality drama. The Arena reopened at Mead Center for American Theater in late 2010, making it the leading center for production, development, and study of American theater.

③ Folger Theatre

Visitors are treated to a rare experience in this Elizabethan-style theater, which strongly suggests the setting in which Shakespeare's works were originally performed. Works of the Bard and his near contemporaries are featured, and performances of medieval and baroque music fill the rich, varied schedule *(see p79)*.

④ Shakespeare Theatre
MAP Q4 ▪ 450 7th St, NW

Top actors, directors, designers, and lighting experts are involved in every dazzling production here. Although specializing in Shakespeare, the company also mounts works by other playwrights.

⑤ Kennedy Center

With works ranging from Shakespeare to Sondheim, from gripping drama and opera to light-hearted comedies and musicals, the many theater productions at this landmark arts center are almost always critically acclaimed. There are a variety of performance spaces catering to different styles, seating from just a few hundred people to more than 2,000 *(see p99)*.

East Terrace at the Kennedy Center

(6) Woolly Mammoth Theatre Company

MAP Q4 ▪ 641 D St, NW ▪ 202-393-3939

Widely acknowledged as the city's most daring theater company, Woolly Mammoth stages new, innovative, and thought-provoking productions.

(7) National Theatre

MAP P4 ▪ 1321 Pennsylvania Ave, NW ▪ 202-628-6161

A wonderful venue that hosts top touring shows, the National Theatre opened in 1835. Since then, a parade of stars and groups such as the Ziegfeld Follies have performed here. Many Broadway classics have staged their premiere here, including *Showboat* and *West Side Story*.

Exterior of the National Theatre

(8) GALA Hispanic Theatre

MAP D3 ▪ 3333 14th St, NW

The recipient of a huge number of awards, this award-winning theater mounts performances in Spanish with simultaneous English translation. Brilliant productions of works from the classical to the absurd attract a diverse audience.

(9) Studio Theatre

MAP P2 ▪ 1501 14th St, NW

Off-Broadway hits, classics, and experimental fare make up the season at this performance landmark with four theater spaces.

(10) Harman Center for the Arts

MAP Q4 ▪ 610 F St, NW

As well as being a 21st-century expanded stage for the Shakespeare Theatre Company, the Harman Center also offers great theater, ballet, and musical performances.

TOP 10 ENTERTAINMENT VENUES

Lisner Auditorium performance

1 Lisner Auditorium
MAP M3 ▪ 21st and H Sts, NW
This university theater features everything from world music to classical orchestras.

2 Warner Theatre
MAP P4 ▪ 13th & E Sts, NW
You'll find Broadway shows, comedians, and concerts here.

3 Carter Barron Amphitheatre
MAP D2 ▪ 4850 Colorado Ave, NW
Open-air stage in Rock Creek Park *(see pp60–61)*. Shows throughout summer.

4 Coolidge Auditorium
MAP S5 ▪ Library of Congress, 10 1st St, SE
The home of the Library of Congress music series *(see p79)*.

5 Capital One Arena
The home of DC's basketball and hockey teams has many attractions beyond the games *(see p95)*.

6 Nationals Park
MAP E4 ▪ 1500 S Capitol St, SE
Home to the Washington Nationals baseball team, this park is a LEED certified green sports stadium.

7 DAR Constitution Hall
MAP N4 ▪ 1776 D St, NW
The largest concert hall in DC.

8 Lincoln Theatre
MAP P1 ▪ 1215 U St, NW
An intimate setting for an eclectic mix of jazz and popular works of theatre.

9 Wolf Trap National Park for the Performing Arts
Metro West Falls Church ▪ 1551 Trap Rd, Vienna, VA
An open-air venue for all the big names in entertainment.

10 Jiffy Lube Live
7800 Cellar Door Drive, Bristow, VA ▪ Rte I-66 to exit 44
International rock stars perform at this open-air arena.

TOP10 Restaurants

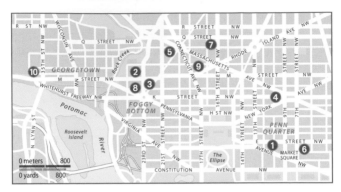

1 Central Michel Richard
Sizeable plates of comfort food, such as braised lamb shanks with spaetzle, small pasta-like dough dumplings *(see p91)*.

2 Blue Duck Tavern
Traditional American fare is served in a contemporary neighborhood tavern *(see p103)*.

West End Bistro

3 West End Bistro
MAP M3 ▪ 1190 22nd St, NW ▪ $$
Located in the Ritz-Carlton, this bistro adds European accents to fine American ingredients.

4 Acadiana
MAP Q3 ▪ 901 New York Ave, NW ▪ $$$
This elegant restaurant offers up modern interpretations of Louisiana dishes by chef Jeff Tunks.

5 Obelisk
MAP N2 ▪ 2029 P St, NW ▪ $$$
Obelisk serves a fixed-price menu of the finest Italian dishes.

6 Rasika
MAP Q4 ▪ 633 D St, NW ▪ $$$
Modern, innovative, and popular Indian fine dining. Dishes include flavorful curries and tandoori (clay oven baked) food. Try the *palak chaat* (crispy baby spinach with sweet yogurt and chutney).

7 Komi
MAP N2 ▪ 1509 17th St, NW ▪ 202-332-9200 ▪ $$$
Reserve well in advance at this much-fêted temple to modern Greek cuisine.

8 Marcel's
Classic French-Belgian fare. Diners can choose one of four *prix-fixe* dinners ranging from four to seven courses *(see p103)*.

9 Iron Gate
MAP N2 ▪ 1734 N St, NW ▪ 202-524-5202 ▪ $$
Mediterranean fare served à la carte, family-style, or as a tasting menu.

10 1789
Federal-style townhouse serving a medley of lamb, oysters, and other dishes *(see p109)*.

For a key to restaurant price ranges see p83

📸 Shopping

1 The Fashion Centre at Pentagon City
MAP C4 ■ 1100 S Hayes St, Arlington, VA 22202

Nordstrom and Macy's are the two anchors here, plus over 170 other stores, a food court, and a spa.

2 National Harbour
MAP D6 ■ Rte I-295 S

On the shores of the Potomac River, and with over 160 retailers, this is one of DC's hottest shopping venues.

3 Friendship Heights
MAP G2

Home to several exclusive retail outlets. Mazza Gallerie is an upscale mall and other stores include Tiffany & Co., Saks Fifth Avenue, and Cartier.

4 Eastern Market
This market is an appetizing source of picnic provisions on weekdays and a carnival of arts and crafts vendors on weekends *(see p81)*.

5 CityCenterDC
MAP P3 ■ 825 10th St, NW

Modern center with high-end shops such as Kate Spade, Dior, and Boss.

6 Potomac Mills Mall
2700 Potomac Mills Circle, Woodbridge, VA

This is one of the largest discount malls in the region.

Georgetown store

7 Georgetown
MAP L2

Probably the most famous shopping area in the city, partly because of the hundreds of shops, but also for the pervasive sense of style.

8 Penn Quarter
MAP Q4 ■ 7th and G Street

This district is filled with restaurants, stores such as Urban Outfitters and Macy's, and small boutiques.

9 Tysons Corner Center and Tysons Galleria
1961 Chain Bridge Rd, McLean, VA & 2001 International Drive, McLean, VA

This huge two-site shopping complex features Cartier, Louis Vuitton, Lord & Taylor, Saks Fifth Avenue, Macy's, and Neiman Marcus.

10 14th and P Street
MAP P2

This gentrified area is filled with galleries, restaurants, boutiques, and stores, especially furniture shops.

Potomac Mills Mall illuminated in the evening light

TOP10 **Washington, DC for Free**

Lionesses basking in the sun at the National Zoological Park

1 Animal Magic
One of the best free places to spend a day outdoors is the National Zoological Park. There are all the usual animals but one of the biggest draws is the giant pandas: Mei Xiang, Tian Tian, and the young cub, Bei Bei (see pp32–3).

2 Architectural Gems
Washington DC's superlative architecture is all around you, but is typified by three very remarkable buildings: the National Archives (see p88); the Library of Congress Jefferson Building (see p79), and Union Station (see p79). You can see the first two on a free guided tour; Union Station is open to all.

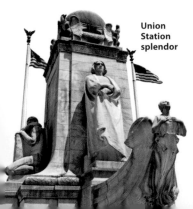

Union Station splendor

3 Children's Theater
The National Theatre offers free kid-oriented Saturday morning entertainment at 9:30am and 11am – tickets are issued 30 minutes beforehand. Shows range from short plays such as Snow White and the Seven Dwarves to magic, puppetry, and music of all sorts (see p67).

4 Lunchtime Music
MAP P4 ■ www.itcdc.com
All summer long, some of the DC's best toe-tapping free music can be found at lunchtime in the Woodrow Wilson Plaza at the Ronald Reagan Building. Top entertainers perform Monday to Friday, offering a variety of music. Pack a picnic lunch or visit the adjacent food court for supplies.

5 Capitol Walking Tour
One of the best freebies in town is the walking tour of the US Capitol building. It melds art and architecture, every element of which celebrates the vision of America's Founding Fathers (see pp12–13).

6 Culture at the Kennedy
The Kennedy Center offers a free performance on the Millennium Stage every day at 6pm. Offerings range from music to dance, poetry, comedy, and theater (see p99).

7 Free Flicks
MAP P5 ▪ www.dcoutdoor
films.com

During the summer, Screen on the Green brings free movies to a giant screen on the National Mall near the Washington Monument. Other outdoor cinema sites include Capitol Hill and Georgetown Waterfront Park. Bring a blanket and snacks (no alcohol) and enjoy the show.

8 Green Escape
The United States Botanical Garden offers a lush, free refuge to Mall-weary visitors. The vast and beautiful conservatory shelters over 4,000 varieties of plants from around the world. Favorite exhibits include the Jungle, the Orchid Collection, and the Children's Garden (see p80).

9 Priceless Plantings
At the 640-acre (260-ha) National Arboretum, walkers and cyclists are free to explore the myriad paths leading to such delights as a hidden pagoda in the Japanese Stroll Garden. From mid-April to May, tens of thousands of azaleas are in bloom (see p60).

National Arboretum

10 Making Money for Free
MAP P5 ▪ 14th and C Sts ▪ 202-874-2330 ▪ Open 8:30am–2:45pm Mon–Fri ▪ www.moneyfactory.gov/washingtondctours.html

One of DC's most popular tours is that of the Bureau of Engraving and Printing, where visitors can goggle at millions of US dollars being printed. Tickets are required from March to August; be at the ticket booth at 8am to be sure of a ticket for that day.

TOP 10 BUDGET TIPS

Washington, DC Metrorail station

1 The Metrorail is fast, efficient, and affordable. Fares are higher during rush hour, so try to time travels for the middle of the day and the evening.

2 Free Tours by Foot offers walking tours in various DC locations. They are not exactly free though – at the end of the tour you are asked to make a donation. See www.freetoursbyfoot.com for tour details.

3 DC street vendors can be pricey. For a low-cost alternative, hit the food court in Union Station (see p79), or the cafeteria at the Capitol Visitor Center (see p13). Better yet, pack a lunch and enjoy it on the Mall.

4 Plan your trip to cover a weekend. On weekends hotel room rates can be as little as half the weekday rates.

5 Look for a hotel that offers a robust free breakfast. It saves you time and the cost of a meal.

6 If you have a car with you, buy your gas outside DC, where it is usually much cheaper.

7 Hotels are also often cheaper in nearby Virginia and Maryland.

8 Check online private rental sites like VRBO (vrbo.com) and Airbnb (airbnb.com). It is possible to find a quality apartment or condominium in a great neighborhood for the about the same price as a discount hotel room.

9 CultureCapital.com sells tickets to a variety of theater, dance and musical performances throughout the city.

10 Check websites and call those attractions that charge admission. They often offer discounts at specific times, or give out coupons that lower admission fees.

TOP 10 Festivals and Cultural Events

Chinese New Year celebrations

1 Chinese New Year
MAP Q3 ■ Chinatown ■ Late Jan–early Feb

New Year is celebrated on a Sunday with special menus at the restaurants, traditional events, a parade, and fireworks. Simply pass through the ornate arch at 7th and H streets, NW to join in the colorful festivities.

2 National Cherry Blossom Festival
MAP N6 ■ Tidal Basin ■ Late Mar–mid-Apr

The lake is surrounded by beautiful Japanese cherry trees, which originated with the 1912 gift of 3,000 specimens to the city by the mayor of Tokyo. The festival celebrating their spring blossoming includes performances, a parade, and such offbeat but appropriate events as a sushi-making contest.

3 Filmfest DC
Citywide ■ Apr ■ www.filmfestdc.org

This top-quality festival has brought the best of world cinema to the city since 1986. The most exciting new films are shown over two weeks at various venues, and discussions and film-oriented events are held at theaters and cafés across town.

4 Washington Nationals
MAP E4 ■ 1500 S Capitol St, SE ■ 888-632-NATS ■ Apr–Oct ■ www.nationals.com

Big-league baseball returned to Washington in 2005 after a 30-year absence. The Washington Nationals fill the stands of the Nationals Park from April to October.

5 Capital Jazz Fest
Merriweather Post Pavilion, Columbia, MD ■ Early Jun ■ www.capitaljazz.com

This annual three-day festival of jazz and blues boasts an impressive line-up of national and international artists and bands.

6 Giant National Capitol Barbecue Battle
MAP P4 ■ Pennsylvania Ave ■ Late Jun ■ www.bbqindc.com

Pennsylvania Avenue is awash with the enticing smell of smoked pork during the annual National Capitol Barbecue Battle. Top barbecue restaurants and pit-masters from around DC and the nation gather to compete for $40,000 in prize money. Visitors get to stroll the five-block-long venue, sampling tasty dishes, enjoying music, cooking demonstrations, and children's activities.

7 Smithsonian Folklife Festival
MAP N5 ■ National Mall ■ Jun–Jul

Fascinating and entertaining cookery, storytelling, craft-making, dancing, music, and art fill the National

Folklife Festival

Mall for two weeks around Independence Day (July 4). This is undoubtedly one of the largest and best cultural events in the world.

8 Shakespeare Free for All

MAP Q4 ▪ 610 F St, NW ▪ Aug ▪ www. shakespearetheatre.org

The last two weeks of August bring free performances by the Shakespeare Theatre Company (see p66) at the Sidney Harman Hall. Tickets are made available by online lottery and at the venue on the day.

9 National Book Festival

MAP Q3 ▪ Washington Convention Center ▪ Sep ▪ www.loc. gov/bookfest

Organized and sponsored by the Library of Congress, this festival is free and open to the public. Around 50 authors of fiction, non-fiction, and children's books give readings, presentations, interviews, and book signings; plus, there are giveaways, promotions, and activities sponsored by leading publishing companies.

National Book Festival

10 Washington National Cathedral Christmas Services

MAP H4 ▪ Massachusetts & Wisconsin Aves, NW ▪ Dec ▪ Adm (some events); check website ▪ www.cathedral.org

The cathedral (see pp30–31) launches the festivities with Handel's Messiah concerts and stunning decorations. Throughout the season, music and concerts are presented, culminating with the elaborate celebrations of Christmas Eve and Christmas Day.

TOP 10 ONE-DAY EVENTS

Blossom Kite Festival

1 Martin Luther King, Jr. Day
Citywide ▪ 3rd Mon in Jan
Church services held. Check local papers for details.

2 President's Day
MAP D5 ▪ 3rd Mon in Feb
Alexandria, VA (see p111) hosts the nation's largest President's Day Parade, and Mount Vernon (see pp36–9) has free admission.

3 St. Patrick's Day
MAP O4 ▪ Constitution Ave, NW ▪ Sun before Mar 17
A parade in honor of St. Patrick's Day.

4 Blossom Kite Festival
MAP N5 ▪ National Mall ▪ Late Mar–early Apr
Competitions include home-built kites, fighting kites, and others.

5 White House Easter Egg Roll
MAP N4 ▪ White House ▪ Easter Mon
Children's activities, music, and egg rolling. Advance tickets only.

6 Memorial Day
Citywide ▪ Last Mon in May
Concerts, ceremonies and a parade on Constitution Avenue honor those who died in the service of their country.

7 Independence Day
MAP N5 ▪ National Mall ▪ Jul 4
The celebration culminates with a musical fireworks display.

8 National Symphony Labor Day Concert
MAP R5 ▪ US Capitol ▪ Labor Day
The official end of summer.

9 International Gold Cup Steeplechase Races
Great Meadows Events Centers, The Plains, VA ▪ Mid-Oct
Races at the peak of the fall foliage.

10 National Christmas Tree Lighting
MAP N4 ▪ The Ellipse ▪ Early Dec
The decorations are joyous.

🔟 Trips from Washington, DC

Vibrant fall colors on the mountains along Skyline Drive, Virginia

1 Baltimore, Maryland
Rte I-95

Called "Charm City" by its residents, Baltimore offers museums of art, industry, baseball, science, railroads, and marine trade along with historic sites from every American period. Its National Aquarium is among the finest in the world. The historic Lexington Market, established in 1782, has over 100 food vendors.

2 Annapolis, Maryland
Rte 50 ▪ William Paca House: 186 Prince George St; open 10am–5pm Mon–Sat, noon–5pm Sun; closed Jan–late Mar ▪ Adm

This enticing city is one of the East Coast's great sailing centers as well as home to the US Naval Academy. The 18th-century home of William Paca, who signed the Declaration of Independence and was later governor of Maryland, is here. Tours of the State Capitol are also popular.

Annapolis, Maryland

3 Skyline Drive, Virginia
Off Rte I-66

This delightful winding road passes 107 miles (170 km) through the mountain and valley scenery of Virginia's Shenandoah National Park. Many hiking trails to isolated peaks, waterfalls, and rare forest environments begin from the main highway.

4 Harpers Ferry, West Virginia
Rte 340

Before the Civil War, John Brown carried out his famous raid against government troops here in Harpers Ferry, protesting the legality of slavery in the United States. This picturesque little town around the old Potomac waterfront has been well preserved and is filled with exhibits about its history.

5 Chincoteague and Assateague, Virginia
Off Rte 13

Assateague Island is famed for its wild ponies. The pony swim and auction, held on the last Wednesday and Thursday of July, is a major tourist attraction. The Chincoteague National Wildlife Refuge, spread across 22 sq miles (57 sq km), is a paradise for bird-watchers and nature buffs. The local seafood is first-rate, and the ice cream made here is justifiably famous.

6 Colonial Williamsburg and Historic Jamestown
Off Rte 1-95 S

Williamsburg was the capital of the fledgling United States during the Revolutionary War. Today, Colonial Williamsburg is the largest living history museum in America, with over 500 reconstructed colonial buildings. Nearby, Jamestown is a reconstruction of the first successful English settlement in America.

Colonial Williamsburg

7 Fredericksburg, Virginia
Rte 1

This city on the Rappahannock River offers colonial homes, moving Civil War sites, and a downtown filled with shops and restaurants. A marked walking tour lays out milestones in the city's history.

8 Frederick, Maryland
Rte I-270

Noted for its majestic bridges, Frederick is a city that is steeped in the memory of 19th-century life and Civil War battles. The city also has an exceptional artistic and cultural life.

Gettysburg statue

9 Manassas Battlefield
Off Rte I-66

This Civil War battlefield is where Confederate and Union soldiers fell by the thousands fighting for conflicting visions of the nation's future. Manassas experienced two pitched battles, the first an opening confrontation of untested troops, the second a bloodbath.

10 Gettysburg, Pennsylvania
Rte 15

The three-day battle of Gettysburg in 1863 was the bloodiest of the Civil War, killing over 51,000. Lincoln famously dedicated the cemetery here. The Gettysburg National Military Park is among the most visited sites on the East Coast.

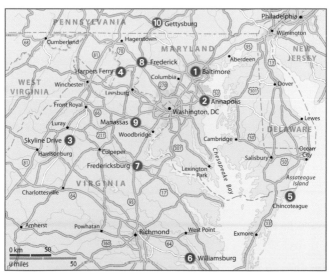

Washington, DC Area by Area

Colorful townhouses in Georgetown

TOP 10 Around Capitol Hill

Folger Shakespeare Library and Theatre

Buzzing with the business of government, Capitol Hill is also a place for shopping, entertainment, food and drink, or simply strolling its handsome neighborhood streets. Approached from the west, the area begins with the meticulously landscaped US Capitol complex, which, as well as the Capitol itself, includes the US Botanic Garden, the Supreme Court Building, and the Library of Congress. Union Station, to the north, is one of the finest railroad terminals in the world.

AROUND CAPITOL HILL

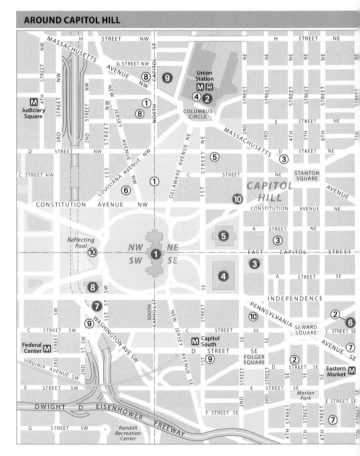

1 US Capitol

Symbolizing both government power and the control of that power by the people, the Capitol crowns the east end of the Mall *(see pp12–15)*.

2 Union Station

MAP R4 ■ 50 Massachusetts Ave, NE

Opened in 1907, this magnificent Beaux Arts building is still a fully functional transportation hub. The lofty barrel-vaulted concourse, decorated with 70 lbs (32 kg) of gleaming gold leaf, is one of the great public spaces in the city – the Washington Monument, laid

Union Station's magnificent interior

on its side, would easily fit within its length. Over 23 million people pass through the station each year.

3 Folger Shakespeare Library and Theatre

MAP S5 ■ 201 East Capitol St, SE ■ 202-544-4600 ■ Open 10am–5pm Mon–Sat, noon–5pm Sun ■ www.folger.edu

The world's largest library of printed editions of Shakespeare's works is at the Folger, and performances at the 16th-century-style theater provide insights into Shakespeare and his times. There is also a huge collection of Renaissance works in other fields, plus playbills, musical instruments, and costumes. The Neo-Classical building, a 1929 design by Paul Philippe Cret, is on the National Register of Historic Places *(see p66)*.

4 Library of Congress

MAP S5 ■ 101 Independence Ave, SE ■ 202-707-5000 ■ Opening hours vary, check website ■ www.loc.gov

The largest collection of books, recordings, and images in the world got its humble start when the US government bought 6,487 books from Thomas Jefferson after fire destroyed the first congressional library in 1814. Free hour-long tours of the spectacular Jefferson Building take in the Italianate-pillared Great Hall; the vast, circular Main Reading Room; a rare Gutenberg Bible; and Jefferson's original book collection.

0 meters 400
0 yards 400

STREET NE

STREET NE

AVENUE NE

MARYLAND AVENUE NE

E STREET NE

D STREET NE

C STREET NE

CONSTITUTION AVENUE NE

NE

④ *Lincoln Park* ⑤

NORTH CAROLINA AVENUE NE

NORTH CAROLINA AVENUE SE

AVENUE SE

SE

SE STREET

8TH 9TH 10TH 11TH 12TH 13TH 14TH STREET

⑥

G ST SE

5 Supreme Court Building
MAP S4 ■ 1st St & East Capitol St, NE ■ 202-479-3030 ■ Open 9am–4:30pm Mon–Fri except federal holidays

The home of the highest seat of the judicial branch of the US government is a handsome Neo-Classical building designed by Cass Gilbert – the American architect who designed the beautiful Woolworth Building in New York City – and completed in 1935. On its west pediment, above the main entrance's marble columns, is inscribed in bold letters the famous motto "Equal Justice Under Law."

6 Eastern Market
MAP S5 ■ 7th St & C St, SE ■ Open 7am–7pm Tue–Fri, 7am–6pm Sat, 9am–5pm Sun

Completed in 1873, Eastern Market was designed by a prominent local architect, Adolph Cluss. Since then, it has served as a neighborhood meeting place and as a fresh food market with produce, cheese, meat, and fish. A variety of prepared food vendors are also popular. On weekends hundreds of local artists and crafters set up booths on the plaza.

7 Bartholdi Park and Fountain
MAP R5 ■ 1st St & Washington Ave, SW ■ www.usbg.gov

This immaculate park is bursting with flowers and ornamental plants. Its symmetrical design radiates out

Bartholdi Park and Fountain

> **CAPITOL HILL RESIDENCES**
>
> In the early 19th century, the area east of the Capitol was filled with a motley collection of boarding houses and taverns where members of Congress stayed during legislative sessions. During the 19th and into the 20th centuries, a diverse mix of housing styles – Federal townhouses, manor houses, Queen Anne, interspersed with two-storey frame dwellings – developed. The protected Capitol Hill Historic District is now the largest historic residential district in the city.

from the fine Gilded Age cast-iron Bartholdi Fountain, a three-storey-high construction of supple human forms, European-style lights, and a non-stop flow of water *(see p61)*.

8 US Botanic Garden
MAP R5 ■ On the Capitol grounds at Maryland Ave & 1st St, SW ■ 202-225-8333 ■ Open 10am–5pm daily ■ www.usbg.gov

Long valued by Capitol Hill residents as a quiet retreat, the Botanic Garden Conservatory is home to some 4,000 living plants that have been arranged into themes and biosystems, such as Plant Adaptations, Tropics, Orchids, and Medicinal Plants. The wedge-shaped National Garden, to the west of the Conservatory, includes glorious colorful outdoor displays. The main court is a wonderfully fragrant spot and a perfect place to sit and rest, and there's a Children's Garden to keep youngsters happy *(see p60)*.

National Postal Museum

9 National Postal Museum
MAP R4 ▪ 2 Massachusetts
Ave, NE ▪ Open 10am–5:30pm daily;
closed Dec 25 ▪ postalmuseum.si.edu

The United States Postal Service
(USPS) delivers over 500 million
items of mail every day, and this fun
museum traces its development
from the days of the Pony Express
onwards (see p58).

10 Belmont-Paul Women's Equality National Monument
MAP S4 ▪ 144 Constitution Ave, NE
▪ 202-546-1210 ▪ Tours 11am–3pm
Thu–Sat ▪ Donation

Built in 1750 and expanded in 1800,
this house is one of the most historic
in Washington. It was the only private
residence burned during the War
of 1812 because Americans fired
on the invading British from here
(see p42). The completely rebuilt
house was bought by the National
Women's Party in 1929 and remains
their home today. Visitors can see
the elaborate but homely period
furnishings, as well as objects and
documents fundamental to the suf-
fragist and feminist movements in
the United States. In 2016 the house
was designated as a US National
Monument (see p49).

A DAY AROUND EASTERN MARKET

Library of Congress
Folger Shakespeare Library and Theatre
The Market Lunch
Eastern Market
The Flea Market at Eastern Market
Woven History
and Silk Road
Eastern Market Metro Station

▶ MORNING

Before a day of shopping, begin
with a bit of history at the Library
of Congress (see p79), a handsome example of the Italian
Renaissance style, with unsur-
passed interiors. The first tour
is at 10:30am.

Turn right onto East Capitol
Street, then right again, and
continue one block to the Folger
Shakespeare Library and Theatre
(see p79). The Elizabethan theater
is enchanting, and the materials
on display are both rare and
fascinating, as are the changing
temporary exhibitions.

Walk east to 7th Street and turn
right. A little over two blocks
farther on is Eastern Market.
On weekends, it is surrounded
by arts and crafts vendors and
flower stalls. The Market Lunch
(see p83) inside is a great choice
for a bite to eat and a rest.

AFTERNOON

If it's a Sunday, spend the
afternoon at the Flea Market at
Eastern Market, on 7th Street
between C and Pennsylvania. It
features 100 or more vendors
selling antiques, Oriental rugs,
fabrics, fine art photographs,
jewelry, and other items. If the
flea market is closed, walk a
block south of Eastern Market
and visit Woven History and Silk
Road (311–5 7th St, SE; 202-543-
1705; open 10am–6pm Tue–Sun)
for its fabrics, rugs, and crafts
from Asia and South America.

To return home from here, turn
right and the Eastern Market
Metro Station is situated directly
ahead of you.

See map on pp78–9 ←

The Best of the Rest

1 Capital Grounds
MAP R4–5

The lovely gardens and walkways that surround the Capitol are the work of renowned landscape designer Frederick Law Olmsted, who created the plan for the grounds in 1874.

2 Ebenezer United Methodist Church
MAP S5 ▪ 420 D St, SE ▪ Open 10am–2pm Mon–Fri

Washington's first congregation of African-American Methodists and Episcopals. It also became home to the first public school for black children after the Emancipation Proclamation.

3 Alleys and Carriageways
MAP S5

The alleys of Capitol Hill, notorious in the 19th century for their squalid and cramped houses, have today been turned into charming little homes.

4 Emancipation Monument
Lincoln Park ▪ Metro Eastern Market

Lincoln holds the Emancipation Proclamation while the last slave, Archer Alexander, breaks his chains *(see p47)*.

5 Statue of Mary McLeod Bethune
Lincoln Park ▪ Metro Eastern Market

This modern sculpture shows the great African-American educator and activist with two African-American children. It symbolizes knowledge handed down through generations *(see p46)*.

6 Robert A. Taft Memorial
MAP R4 ▪ Constitution Ave & 1st St, NW ▪ 202-226-8000 ▪ Open 24 hrs daily

This memorial opposite the Capitol honors Senator Taft for his honesty and courage. The carillon in the 100-ft- (30-m-) tall bell tower plays every 15 minutes.

7 Christ Church
MAP S6 ▪ 620 G St, SE

This elegant church, built in 1805, had many prominent parishioners, including presidents Jefferson, Madison, and Monroe.

8 National Guard Memorial Museum
MAP R4 ▪ 1 Massachusetts Ave, NW ▪ 202-408-5887 ▪ Open 9am–4pm Mon–Fri

This gallery remembers citizens who gave their lives to protect the nation.

9 American Veterans Disabled for Life Memorial
MAP R5 ▪ 150 Washington Ave, SW

This plaza-like oasis is dedicated to disabled veterans. It features a tree-shaded, star-shaped pool and interpretive glass and bronze panels.

10 Ulysses S. Grant Memorial
US Capitol ▪ MAP R5

This equestrian grouping honors the Union victory in the Civil War. Sculptor Henry Shrady (1871–1922) took 20 years to complete the work *(see p51)*.

Ulysses S. Grant Memorial

Places to Eat

① Dubliner Restaurant
MAP R4 ▪ 4 F Street ▪ 202-737-3773 ▪ $

An Irish pub with free-flowing pints and good hearty food. Try the steak and fries or the shepherd's pie. There is live Irish music from 9pm and the outdoor patio is perfect for warm summer evenings.

② The Market Lunch
MAP S5 ▪ Eastern Market, 225 7th St ▪ 202-547-8444 ▪ No credit cards ▪ $

This breakfast and lunch counter, with nearby tables, serves burgers and sandwiches, with a specialty in seafood. Try the crabcakes and oyster sandwiches. Breakfast and weekend brunch are very popular. No alcohol.

③ Café Berlin
MAP S4 ▪ 322 Massachusetts Ave, NE ▪ 202-543-7656 ▪ $

A German restaurant in a townhouse setting. *Wiener schnitzel*, pork loin with sauerkraut, and other hearty dishes are on the menu. The desserts are very tempting.

④ Shake Shack
MAP R5 ▪ 50 Massachusetts Ave, NE ▪ 202-684-2428 ▪ $

Located in Union Station's West Hall, this popular eatery serves breakfast as well as a selection of burgers, hot dogs, fries, and shakes.

⑤ The Monocle
MAP S4 ▪ 107 D St, NE ▪ 202-546-4488 ▪ $$

The Monocle claims to be the first fine-dining restaurant on Capitol Hill. A favorite with the Kennedys, it's still popular with the power-dining crowd

A table at the Monocle

and is known for its well-hung steaks and ocean-fresh seafood.

⑥ Ambar
MAP S5 ▪ 523 8th St SE ▪ 202-813-3039 ▪ $$

Traditional yet modern Balkan fare with an eclectic variety of small plates and East European wines.

⑦ Le Pain Quotidien
MAP S5 ▪ 660 Pennsylvania Ave, SE ▪ 202-459-9147 ▪ $

A branch of the ubiquitous Belgian chain of light bite bakery cafés – the name means "daily bread."

⑧ Bistro Bis
MAP R4 ▪ 15 E St, NW ▪ 202-661-2700 ▪ $$

A modern take on a French bistro with a stylish cherry-wood interior; deservedly popular.

⑨ Tortilla Coast
MAP R5 ▪ 400 1st St, SE ▪ 202-546-6768 ▪ $

Come here for some great Tex-Mex food. George W. Bush was said to be a customer here before he was elected president.

⑩ Sonoma
MAP S5 ▪ 223 Pennsylvania Ave, SE ▪ 202-544-8088 ▪ $$

On offer at Sonoma are California cuisine, cheese platters, and an eclectic menu of wines.

See map on pp78–9 ←

▣ The Mall and Federal Triangle

Even Washingtonians whose daily life rarely takes them to the National Mall regard this magnificent grassy park as the heart of the city. It stretches 2.5 miles (4 km) from the Capitol to the Potomac River, just beyond the Lincoln Memorial. Alongside and nearby are key symbols of the city and the nation: memorials to past suffering and triumphs, the workplaces of the federal government, and the Smithsonian museums. The Mall also serves as a national public square – it fills to capacity for the dazzling Fourth of July fireworks, and bustles daily with ordinary people jogging, strolling, or just enjoying the extraordinary views.

National Museum of American History

THE MALL AND FEDERAL TRIANGLE

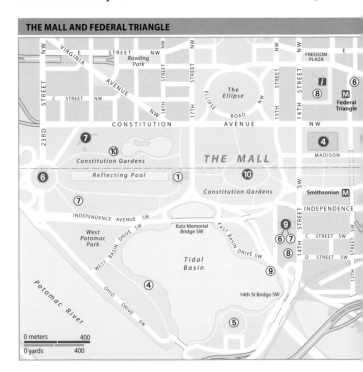

1 National Gallery of Art

Stroll through this building surrounded by illustrious artworks dating from before the Renaissance to the current day. The sculpture garden is a hit for its outdoor setting, summer jazz concerts, a winter ice-skating rink, and café (see pp24–7).

The modern exterior of the National Museum of the American Indian

2 National Museum of the American Indian

MAP Q5 ■ 4th St at Independence Ave, SW ■ Open 10am–5:30pm daily

This museum enshrines 10,000 years of Native American life and culture, and acknowledges the place of native peoples in the history of the Americas. The collection includes over 800,000 items, 7,000 of which are on display. Exhibits include pre-Columbian gold figurines, beadwork, textiles, and pottery from the Arctic to Patagonia. The building itself has been designed in harmony with Native American beliefs. The entrance faces east and light spills into the museum, reflecting the importance of the sun in American Indian culture (see p54).

3 National Air and Space Museum

The story of flight, one of the most stirring in human history, is powerfully depicted in this favorite museum, renowned for its collection of precious artifacts of the challenging experience of flying (see pp20–21).

4 National Museum of American History

The story of the United States of America, from its beginnings to the present day, is told here through public icons and examinations of the daily lives of ordinary people. The many permanent exhibits include Julia Child's TV kitchen; Inventing in America; the Star-Spangled Banner Gallery; and "America on the Move," looking at modes of transport from 1876 to today (see pp22–3).

5 Hirshhorn Museum and Sculpture Garden

MAP Q5 ■ 7th St at Independence Ave, SW ■ 202-633-4674 ■ Open 10am–5:30pm daily; closed Dec 25

The Hirshhorn Museum's focus is on international contemporary, modern and up-and-coming art, with exceptional holdings and exhibitions. The unusual circular building, which dates from 1974, provides a striking setting for outdoor sculpture in the surrounding plaza. Another sculpture garden across Jefferson Drive displays over 60 pieces of large-scale works of art (see p56).

The magnificent Lincoln Memorial and Reflecting Pool

6 Lincoln Memorial
MAP M5 ■ 23rd St, NW & Independence Ave ■ Open 24 hours

This imposing marble memorial honors the US president who shepherded the country through its most difficult era. Designed by Henry Bacon (1866–1924) and featuring a monumental 19-ft- (6-m-) high statue of the seated Lincoln by Daniel Chester French (1850–1931), the memorial was dedicated in 1922. The Greek architecture reflects the ideals of its time *(see p50)*.

7 Vietnam Veterans Memorial
MAP M5 ■ Constitution Ave & 21st St, NW ■ Open 24 hours

This stark memorial features a black polished wall on which are inscribed the names of those who died during the Vietnam War. Controversial when it was opened, because of its minimalism and because it failed to glorify the war, the memorial has become one of the most popular in the world. Its creator, the Chinese-American Maya Lin, was a 21-year-old student when she designed it. More traditional statues were added in 1984 *(see pp50–51)*.

Vietnam Veterans Memorial

THE FEDERAL TRIANGLE

The area now known as the Federal Triangle was developed during Franklin D. Roosevelt's administration and improved by John F. Kennedy. Before then, the three-sided site, between 6th and 14th Streets and Pennsylvania and Constitution Avenues NW, was a run-down area. Its main buildings are the Federal Trade Commission, the National Archives, the Department of Justice, the Internal Revenue Service, and the R. Reagan Building and International Trade Center.

---

8 National Museum of Natural History

A favorite with children, yet filled with fascinating displays and artifacts that appeal to everyone, the vast halls of this Smithsonian museum have everything from the tiny bones of a snake to a giant ritual statue from Easter Island. Other exhibits include the vast Mammal Hall, Pacific Island canoes, fabulous gemstones (including the Hope Diamond), a giant squid, a set from a Chinese opera, and an Egyptian mummy case *(see pp28–9)*.

9 United States Holocaust Memorial Museum
MAP P5 ■ 100 Raoul Wallenberg Place, SW (14th St between C St & Independence Ave) ■ 202-488-0400 ■ Open 10am–5:20pm daily; closed Yom Kippur, Dec 25 ■ www.ushmm.org

Among the city's most challenging sites, this museum is both a working study center for issues relating to the Holocaust and a national memorial for the millions murdered by the World War II Nazi government. The museum is solemn and respectful yet engrossing and highly informative. Free timed passes are required, from March to September, to view the three-storey permanent exhibition. Passes can be obtained at the museum on the day of visit, or in advance online. There are some special exhibitions that can be seen without passes (see pp54–5).

(10) Washington Monument

MAP P5 ■ 15th St between Independence & Constitution Aves ■ Open 9am–5pm daily (to 10pm in summer) ■ Entry by timed ticket

The plain Egyptian design of this radiant spire was largely the result of congressional cost-cutting, but now it seems an inspired choice. At 555 ft (165 m), the monument, built to honor the first president of the United States, towers over everything in the neighborhood and is ringed by 50 flags representing the 50 states of America. As a result of damage caused by a 5.8-magnitude earthquake in August 2011, the monument was closed for 32 months, reopening in May 2014. Visitors can now once more ascend by elevator to the 500-ft (152-m) high viewing deck for breathtaking views over the city.

Washington Monument

A MORNING WALK BY THE WATERFRONT

(▶) Begin your walk at the **Franklin D. Roosevelt Memorial** (see p50) on West Basin Drive. There are hop-on-hop-off tour bus and trolley stops (see p124) directly in front (parking is limited). The sweep of this memorial carries visitors past waterscapes punctuated by engravings of the words of the president and evocative sculptures of his times.

On the left, leaving the memorial, is the little Japanese pagoda given to the city as a gesture of friendship by the mayor of Yokohama in 1958. Graceful Japanese cherry trees line the Tidal Basin bank beyond (see p72). Continue east across Inlet Bridge. About five minutes along the walkway stands the brilliant **Jefferson Memorial** (see p50), noted for its delicate design in spite of its size. Looking out from the steps here to the city is a wonderful experience.

Continue around the waterfront, cross Outlet Bridge, and bear to the left to the little boathouse, where you can rent paddle boats for a unique view of the Tidal Basin (open 10am–6pm daily; last boats out at 5pm; adm). If you prefer to stay on dry land, continue north toward the **Washington Monument** and cross Maine Avenue leading to Raoul Wallenberg Place. On the right is the **United States Holocaust Memorial Museum**. Before taking in the exhibits, gird yourself with some kosher fare in the **Museum Café** (see p91). Then spend the afternoon in remembrance of lives tragically lost under the Nazi regime before (●) and during World War II.

See map on pp84–5 ←

The Best of the Rest

World War II Memorial

1 World War II Memorial
MAP N5 ▪ National Mall

This memorial includes 12 bas-relief sculptures depicting America at war (see p51).

2 Enid A. Haupt Garden
MAP P5 ▪ 10th St & Independence Ave, NW ▪ Open Memorial Day–Sep: 7am–7pm daily; Oct–Memorial Day: 7am–5:45pm daily

These formal gardens are designed to reflect the Smithsonian galleries above which they stand (see p60).

3 National Archives of the United States
MAP Q4 ▪ 700 Pennsylvania Ave, NW ▪ 202-357-5000 ▪ Open 10am–5:30pm daily (to 7pm in summer)

Home to foundation documents of the nation, including the Declaration of Independence (see p55).

4 Franklin D. Roosevelt Memorial
MAP N6 ▪ 900 Ohio Dr, SW

The monument depicts events during the Great Depression and World War II while FDR served as president (see p50).

5 Jefferson Memorial
MAP N6 ▪ Tidal Basin

Words taken from the Declaration of Independence are engraved on the wall here (see p50).

6 Old Post Office Pavilion
MAP P4 ▪ For Clock Tower tours see www.nps.gov/opot/planyourvisit/index.htm

The Old Post Office Pavilion has been transformed into the Trump International Hotel, Washington, DC. The pavilion's old tower is again open to the public (see p49).

7 Korean War Veterans Memorial
MAP M5 ▪ 21st St & Independence Ave, SW

The 19 steel sculptures in this memorial to the 1953 Korean "police action" evoke the realities of war.

8 Bureau of Engraving and Printing
MAP P5 ▪ 14th St at C St, SW ▪ 202-874-2330 ▪ www.moneyfactory.org for tour info ▪ Open 8:30am–2:45pm Mon–Fri

See millions of dollars being printed as you walk along the gallery.

9 National Museum of African Art
MAP Q5 ▪ 950 Independence Ave, SW ▪ Open 10am–5:30pm daily; closed Dec 25

A program of changing exhibitions highlights a diverse collection of African pieces (see p57).

10 Constitution Gardens
MAP N5 ▪ National Mall

This 50-acre (20-ha) park's lovely centerpiece is an island in a tranquil lake, where markers honor the 56 signers of the US Constitution.

Constitution Gardens

Items in Museum Stores

1 American History Themes
The shops at the National Museum of American History (see pp22–3) offer a wide variety of merchandise inspired by museum exhibits. These include personalized dog tags, Star-Spangled Banner themed items, and pop-culture accessories.

2 Jackie Kennedy Jewels
Who needs the real thing when reproductions of Jackie's most famous pieces can be purchased for next to nothing at the museum store at the National Museum of American History (see pp22–3).

3 All Things Dinosaur
You will find lots of dinosaur merchandise for sale, including the Smithsonian book Dinosaur!, in the National Museum of Natural History (see pp28–9).

4 Geodes and Fossils
The Gem and Mineral store in the National Museum of Natural History (see pp28–9) has beautiful examples of geodes – sparkling crystals grown within hollows of other stones – and of fossils embedded in various matrixes.

5 Leather Flight Jackets
Good-quality leather jackets recreate the genuine flying jackets, and the selection and prices are reasonable. In the National Air and Space Museum (see pp20–21).

6 Native American Art
Sculptures, carvings, ceramic pots, and plates created in intricate Native American designs can be purchased at the Museum of the American Indian (see p85).

7 NASA Space Suits
Miniature orange suits, created with care and precise attention to detail, are available for little astronauts at the National Air and Space Museum (see pp20–21).

Whistler's *Symphony in White, No. 1: The White Girl* in the National Gallery

8 National Gallery Prints
Many of the National Gallery's favorite paintings are available as quality prints, as well as in other forms ranging from phone cases to tote bags (see pp24–7).

9 Cherry Blossom Kimono Jacket
Gorgeous satin kimono jackets and scarves are among the magnificent fabric creations available at DC's two fine Asian museum stores. They also have unusual novelties such as a peacock jewelry box (see p57).

10 Handmade Crafts
The George Washington University Museum and the Textile Museum's (see p99) beautiful range of shawls and scarves, vibrant handbags, felt dolls, and inspiring textile-related books all make lovely gifts.

See map on pp84–5

Children's Attractions

1 Lockheed Martin IMAX Theater

Take a space walk, learn about the history of the cosmos, or enjoy one of the immersive 3D experiences here. This National Air and Space Museum theater has a dual 4k laser projection system with enhanced audio systems (see pp20–21).

2 Smithsonian Carousel

MAP P5 ■ 900 Jefferson Dr, SW ■ Open 10am–5pm daily weather permitting ■ Adm

This lovely carousel with its fancifully carved steeds is a treat for young and old alike. The sounds of the band organ are very cheering.

3 Live Insect Zoo

Live arthropods scamper and creep in this section of the Museum of Natural History – some can also be held (see pp28–9).

4 "How Things Fly"

Highly interactive exhibits and scheduled demonstrations at the National Air and Space Museum explain the principles that make flight possible. Kids can understand natural animal flight and human flight in contraptions from balloons to the space shuttle (see pp20–21).

5 imagiNATIONS Activity Center

Hands-on activities at the National Museum of the American Indian (see p85) include basket weaving, learning how snowshoes work, and exploring a full-sized tipi.

6 Daniel's Story, US Holocaust Museum

This exhibition, intended for children aged eight and older, is based on the actual experience of children during the Holocaust. It recounts the story of one young German-Jewish boy's life between 1933 and 1945 (see pp86–7).

7 Einstein Planetarium

Astronomy is kid-friendly at the National Air and Space Museum in the 25-minute film One World, One Sky: Big Bird's Adventure. At 10:30am daily either The Stars Tonight, What's New In Space Science, or One World, One Sky are shown for free. Book tickets in advance (see pp20–21).

8 Live Butterfly Pavilion

This oasis with live butterflies and exotic plants from around the world is a timed-entry area in the National Museum of Natural History (see pp28–9). Entry is free on Tuesday on a first-come first-served basis.

9 Paddle the Tidal Basin

When the kids get tired of museums, head to the Tidal Basin to rent a paddle boat. A leisurely trip around the basin will take you past Franklin D. Roosevelt's tree-lined memorial and the stately Jefferson Memorial (see p88).

10 Ice Skating

The fountain in the National Gallery of Art Sculpture Garden (see p27) is frozen especially for ice skating in the winter, and visitors can rent skates on site.

Ice skating at the National Gallery of Art

See map on p84–5

Lunch Spots

PRICE CATEGORIES
For a three-course meal for one with half
a bottle of wine (or equivalent meal),
taxes and extra charges.

$ under $50 $$ $50–100 $$$ over $100

① Cascade Café & Gelato Bar

MAP Q4 ■ 3rd–9th Sts at Constitution
Ave, NW ■ 202-712-7458 ■ $

Set behind a glass wall in the city's
National Gallery of Art *(see pp24–5)*
concourse Is a man-made waterfall.
Facing this view is an attractive café
that serves up a wide range of hot
and cold food.

② Paul Bakery and Café

MAP Q4 ■ 801 Pennsylvania
Ave, NW ■ 202-524-4500 ■ $

An outlet of the famous French
bakery, this café offers a wide
variety of sandwiches, snacks,
desserts, and organic breads.

③ Pavilion Café

MAP Q4 ■ 3rd–9th Sts at
Constitution Ave, NW ■ 202 289
3361 ■ $

Sandwiches, salads, pizzas, and
a variety of desserts are served
in the Sculpture Garden at the
National Gallery of Art.

④ Garden Café

MAP Q4 ■ 3rd–9th Sts at
Constitution Ave, NW ■ 202-842-
6716 ■ $

This little restaurant in the National
Gallery of Art has the choice of a
good buffet or a traditional à la carte
menu. Surroundings of greenery
combine with lofty ceilings.

⑤ The Source

MAP Q4 ■ 575 Pennsylvania
Ave, NW ■ 202-637-6100 ■ $$

An Asian-influenced menu. The
three-course, fixed-price lunch
menu is recommended. Enjoy a
casual dining atmosphere at this
Newseum location.

Mitsitam Café

⑥ Mitsitam Café

MAP Q5 ■ National Museum
of the American Indian, 4th St &
Independence Ave, SW ■ 202-633-
1000 ■ $

The name means "Let's eat" in
Piscataway. The menu is inspired
by Native American cuisine.

⑦ United States Holocaust Memorial Museum

The Museum Café serves traditional,
kosher, and contemporary American
favorites *(see pp86–7)*.

⑧ Reagan International Trade Center Food Court

MAP Q4 ■ 1300 Pennsylvania Ave,
NW ■ 202-312-1300 ■ $

This large food court has Texas grill,
sushi, and stir-fry as specialties.
Photo ID is required for adults to
enter the building.

⑨ Central Michel Richard

MAP P4 ■ 1001 Pennsylvania
Ave, NW ■ 202-626-0015 ■ $$

Celebrity chef Michel Richard serves
up French flavors and American
concoctions such as lobster burgers
and faux foie gras.

⑩ Atrium Café

The Museum of Natural
History's café serves great grills,
pizzas, and deli sandwiches using
organic ingredients *(see pp28–9)*.

Following pages World War II Memorial

⓾ Penn Quarter

Lincoln's carriage at Ford's Theatre

Like other urban downtown areas, Washington's city center is filled with shops, hotels, restaurants, and theaters for every taste. Yet downtown Washington borders Pennsylvania Avenue – often called "America's main street." This is the direct route between the White House and the Capitol, and is therefore rich in historic associations. Presidential inauguration parades sweep down the avenue every four years; citizens protest here; President Lincoln was shot and died nearby. Washington's importance to world culture is reflected in the ease with which local restaurants and stores cater to an international clientele. The area draws visitors to the attractions of Chinatown, the Capital One Arena, and the feeling of being at the center of the political world.

PENN QUARTER

1 **Top 10 Sights**
see pp95–6

1 **Places to Eat**
see p97

0 meters 400
0 yards 400

The Great Hall of the National Building Museum

1 National Building Museum

MAP Q4 ■ 401 F St, NW ■ Open 10am–5pm Mon–Sat, 11am–5pm Sun ■ Adm ■ www.nbm.org

This grand structure would be a fabulous place to visit even if it were empty. Its eight massive interior columns are among the largest in the world, and its immense interior space has beautiful natural light. The museum is dedicated to document-ing and displaying themes in the art and craft of building. It has perma-nent exhibitions on Washington city and on art created from tools, and mounts temporary exhibitions on topics such as the growth of urban transit and the development of architectural and construction methods. Other exhibits highlight the work of individual prominent archi-tects. Families with young children will particularly enjoy the Building Zone, where they can build towers and drive toy bulldozers.

Booth's Derringer pistol

2 Ford's Theatre

MAP Q4 ■ 511 10th St, NW ■ 202-347-4833 ■ Open 9am–4:30pm daily ■ Timed tickets; adm for advance bookings ■ www.fords.org

John Wilkes Booth shot President Abraham Lincoln in a balcony box here on April 14, 1865 – a tragic event that has made Ford's Theatre one of America's best-known historical sites. A museum contains Booth's .44 caliber Derringer pistol and other objects alongside inter-esting information about President Lincoln and the assassination plot. The restored building also hosts theater productions. Directly across 10th Street is Petersen House, where Lincoln died after being carried from the theater *(see p66)*.

3 Capital One Arena

MAP Q4 ■ 601 F St, NW

While the Capital One Arena is principally a sports arena, it has also become an unofficial community center. It draws crowds night after night with college and professional sports events, big-name concerts, circuses, figure-skating perform-ances, and other events *(see p67)*.

4 Newseum

MAP P4 ■ 555 Pennsylvania Ave, NW ■ 202-292-6100 ■ Open 9am–5pm Mon–Sat, 1–5pm Sun; closed Thanksgiving, Dec 25, Jan 1 ■ Adm ■ www.newseum.org

This museum holds an awe-inspiring dissection of 500 years of the press. Visitors are able to compare media freedoms in 190 countries and view enlarged front pages from around the world that are updated daily. The 9/11 and Pulitzer Prize photography galleries are particularly moving. An unmissable museum experience in the city *(see p55)*.

5 National Museum of Women in the Arts

MAP P3 ▪ 1250 New York Ave, NW ▪ 202-783-5000 ▪ Open 10am–5pm Mon–Sat, noon–5pm Sun; closed Thanksgiving, Dec 25, Jan 1 ▪ Adm

The collection of works by female artists here is among the best in the world, and ranges from Italian artist Lavinia Fontana's *Portrait of a Noblewoman* (c.1580) to Mexican artist Frida Kahlo's 1937 *Self-Portrait Dedicated to Leon Trotsky* (see p57).

6 US Navy Memorial

MAP Q4 ▪ 701 Pennsylvania Ave, NW ▪ Open 9:30am–5pm daily

The centerpiece of this delightful public space is a granite floor – a huge map of the world surrounded by fountains. A statue, dubbed "The Lone Sailor," overlooks the expanse. A free movie, *At Sea*, shows daily.

7 Smithsonian American Art Museum

MAP Q4 ▪ 8th & F Sts, NW ▪ 202-633-1000 ▪ Open 11:30am–7pm daily; closed Dec 25 ▪ www. americanart.si.edu

US Navy Memorial

This large and inclusive collection consists of works by a range of renowned American artists. These include Georgia O'Keefe, Winslow Homer, John Singleton Copley, and many others. Exhibits include the "American Experience," "Art Since 1945," and "Graphic Arts."

8 International Spy Museum

MAP Q4 ▪ 800 F St, NW ▪ 202-393-7798 ▪ Opening hours vary, check website ▪ Adm ▪ www.spymuseum.org

More than just an excellent collection of spy gadgets from around the world, the Spy Museum encourages visitors of all ages to adopt a cover

> **PENNSYLVANIA AVENUE**
>
> When the federal government moved to the city in 1800, Pennsylvania Avenue was selected as the "main street" because the area to the south was too muddy after rains, and the avenue offered a direct route from the President's House to the Capitol – at that time the only substantial buildings in town.

identity and learn how to react to real espionage challenges using interactive displays.

9 National Portrait Gallery

MAP Q4 ▪ 8th & F Sts, NW ▪ Open 11:30am–7pm daily

The ornate 1836 building is a masterpiece in itself. The gallery celebrates remarkable Americans through visual and performing arts. Permanent exhibitions focus on individuals who have helped to shape the country's culture, from presidents and poets to villains and activists. The spectacular waved glass cover over the courtyard is by renowned architect Norman Foster (see p56).

10 Chinatown

MAP Q3 ▪ 7th & H Sts, NW

Although sadly diminished, some vestiges of Chinese culture can still be found among the upscale bars, restaurants, and shops here. Look out for the Friendship Arch which marks the center, with seven pagoda-style roofs ornamented with 300 dragons.

Chinatown

Places to Eat

1 Proof
MAP Q3 ■ 775 G St, NW ■ 202-737-7663 ■ $$$

Wine-lovers are drawn to this downtown hotspot known for its creative modern cuisine and a wine list of over 1,000 different varieties, including 40 that can be served by the glass.

2 Jaleo
MAP Q4 ■ 480 7th St, NW ■ 202-628-7949 ■ $$

A fine tapas restaurant, Jaleo draws rave reviews for its eggplant flan and sautéed shrimp. The atmosphere is always lively, with great music and plenty of sangria.

3 Old Ebbitt Grill
MAP P4 ■ 675 15th St, NW ■ 202-347-4800 ■ $

Founded in 1856, this is the oldest saloon in the city, serving great hamburgers and seasonal entrées. Oyster bar in season.

4 Rosa Mexicano
MAP Q4 ■ 575 7th St, NW ■ 202-783-5522 ■ $$

"Mexican Pink" is a small national chain that serves upscale Mexican food, including an outstanding guacamole (made at the table in a traditional lava-rock mortar) and excellent cocktails.

5 Elephant and Castle
MAP P4 ■ 1201 Pennsylvania Ave, NW ■ 202-347-7707 ■ $

Traditional British comfort food is served here in a homey pub-style atmosphere: the roast-beef-filled Yorkshire puddings, sausage and mash, and shepherd's pie are among the perenniel favorites.

Brasserie Beck

6 Brasserie Beck
MAP Q3 ■ 1101 K St, NW ■ 202-408-1717 ■ $$

A paradise for beer-lovers, Beck offers several varieties and a large French–Belgian menu.

7 Full Kee
MAP Q3 ■ 509 H St, NW ■ 202-371-2233 ■ $

This popular Chinatown Cantonese restaurant serves outstanding soups at an open station.

8 Oyamel Cocina Mexicana
MAP Q4 ■ 401 7th St, NW ■ 202-628-1005 ■ $$

Traditional *antonjitos* and great cocktails at this Mexican eatery.

9 Tony Cheng's Mongolian Restaurant
MAP Q4 ■ 619 H St, NW ■ 202-371-8669 ■ $

The ground floor of this restaurant focuses on Mongolian-style barbecue while Cantonese cuisine and dim sum are served upstairs.

10 District Chophouse and Brewery
MAP Q4 ■ 509 7th St, NW ■ 202-347-3434 ■ $$

Hearty, meaty menus and on-site handcrafted ales cater to sports fans from the Capital One Arena.

See map on p94

TOP 10 The White House and Foggy Bottom

Bust of JFK, Kennedy Center

The majestic White House clearly defines this part of the city – many government buildings stand in the vicinity, including the old and new Executive Office Buildings, the Federal Reserve Building, and the State and Treasury Departments. To the west lies Foggy Bottom, a former swamp area now home to George Washington University. Farther west, the Kennedy Center stands on the Potomac waterfront. Throughout the area, as one would expect, restaurants, hotels, and stores provide the exceptional quality of service required by high-profile diplomats and politicians.

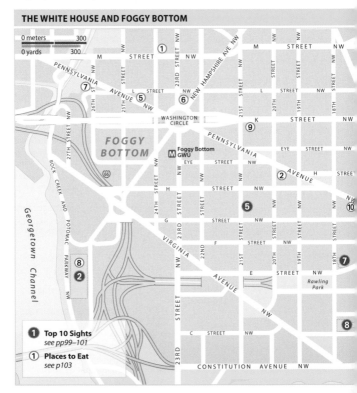

THE WHITE HOUSE AND FOGGY BOTTOM

- **1** Top 10 Sights
  see pp99–101
- **1** Places to Eat
  see p103

1 The White House

Beautiful from any angle, the White House is a symbol of US political power and of democracy throughout the world *(see pp16–19)*.

2 Kennedy Center

MAP M4 ■ 2700 F St, NW ■ 202-467-4600

A memorial to President John F. Kennedy, this massive performance complex – the largest in the country – presents the very best expressions of the artistic culture he loved so well. Here, national and international stars present performances of opera, classical music, musical comedy, drama, jazz, dance, and ballet. Located overlooking the Potomac, its terraces and rooftop restaurant offer spectacular views of the city below *(see p66)*.

3 St. John's Church

MAP N3 ■ 1525 H St, NW ■ Open 9am–3pm Mon–Sat ■ Tours after the Sunday service (summer: 10:30am, winter: 11am) ■ www. stjohns-dc.org

This lovely yellow Episcopalian Church, located on the north side of Lafayette Square, was designed by Benjamin Latrobe and conducted its first service in 1816. From James Madison to Donald Trump, every president of the United States has attended a service at St. John's. The cast iron bell in the steeple was cast by Joseph Revere, son of American Revolution patriot Paul, in 1822. The 25 stained-glass windows, designed and created by Lorin Stained Glass Windows of Chartres, France, were installed in 1885.

4 Renwick Gallery

MAP N3 ■ 1661 Pennsylvania Ave, NW ■ 202-633-7970 ■ Open 10am–5:30pm daily ■ renwick. americanart.si.edu

With its collections of fine American craft works and art, and having undergone extensive renovations, this Smithsonian museum is a gem. The second-floor Grand Salon served as a ballroom and site for special events when the Corcoran Gallery was located here before 1897. Named after its architect, James Renwick, Jr., the 1859 structure is a marvelous Second Empire-style building *(see p56)*.

5 The George Washington University Museum and The Textile Museum

MAP M3 ■ 21st and G St, NW ■ Opening times vary, check website ■ Adm ■ www.museum.gwu.edu

The museum includes the Albert H. Small Washingtoniana Collection of historic Washington, DC documents, and the Textile Museum Collection of over 19,000 objects spanning 5,000 years. The fine Islamic, Peruvian, Pre-Columbian, and Coptic textiles and Oriental carpets are recognized as one of the world's foremost specialized museum collections.

GEORGE WASHINGTON UNIVERSITY

For the last 50 years, GWU has been a major presence in Foggy Bottom, contributing to its diversity and filling its streets with the energy of young students. Founded as Columbian College in 1821, the school adopted its current name in 1904 to honor the wishes expressed by Washington (**below**) for the establishment of a major university in the city.

6 Treasury Building

MAP P4 ▪ 1500 Pennsylvania Ave, NW ▪ Tours currently only available for citizens and legal residents of the US, by appt only ▪ www.treasury.gov

The ornate Greek-Revival style of this building, designed in 1833, suggests a Temple of Money, and its imposing interior design confirms the seriousness with which the republic has always treated its currency. The restored Salmon P. Chase Suite and the Andrew Johnson Office reflect the gravity of official actions during and after the Civil War. The burglar-proof vault is always a hit with visitors, not least because of the beauty of its cast-iron walls and its demonstration of the lower security needs of a simpler time (see p49).

7 The Octagon Museum

MAP N4 ▪ 1799 New York Ave ▪ 202-626-7439 ▪ Open 1–4pm Thu–Sat

This unique and graceful building houses the oldest architecture museum in the country. It was designed by William Thornton, the original architect of the US Capitol Building, as a second home for John Tayloe III, a wealthy friend of George Washington. The house was completed in 1801 – one of the first private residences to be built to Pierre L'Enfant's plan – and provided shelter to President James Madison and his family while workers were rebuilding the White House after its destruction during the War of 1812. The exhibitions of the museum focus on the early Federal period of architecture, principally from 1800 to 1830.

8 Daughters of the American Revolution

MAP N4 ▪ 1776 D St, NW ▪ 202-628-1776 ▪ Museum: open 8:30am–4pm Mon–Fri, 9am–5pm Sat; closed federal holidays

The largest concert hall in the city is in Constitution Hall, the grand performance space operated by the Daughters of the American Revolution (DAR). The cornerstone of this John Russell Pope design was laid in 1928, using the same trowel

Treasury Building

George Washington used for the US Capitol building cornerstone in 1793. The DAR also contains a fascinating museum of early American artifacts, ranging from a simple 17th-century dwelling to an elaborate Victorian parlor. The DAR is also a volunteer women's service promoting patriotism, history, and education – any woman who can prove lineal descent from a patriot of the American Revolution is eligible to join.

9 Lafayette Park
MAP N3 ■ H St between 15th and 17th Sts, NW

In DC's early years, this park served as a slave market, a racetrack, a zoo, and a graveyard. Today, it overlooks the North Portico of the White House, making it a favorite spot for TV news broadcasts, as well as a popular venue for protests and celebrations. The park and its surrounding buildings are a National Historic Landmark District. Of its five statues, the central one is of US President Andrew Jackson on his horse. The others, located in the four corners of the park, are of foreign heroes who fought in the Revolution, including France's General Marquis Gilbert de Lafayette.

Statue in Lafayette Park

10 National Geographic Museum
MAP N3 ■ 17th & M Sts, NW ■ 202-857-7588 ■ Open 10am–6pm daily; closed Thanksgiving, Dec 25 ■ Adm

The first-class exhibits at the National Geographic Museum cover foreign cultures, nature, archeology, and *National Geographic*'s signature breathtaking photography. Superb displays immerse visitors in their subject matter, all reflecting the diversity of our ever-changing planet.

A DAY EXPLORING 17TH STREET, NW

MORNING

Begin your day admiring the interiors at **St. John's Church** *(see p99)*. Next, walk west to **Decatur House** *(see p48)*, a gorgeous Neo-Classical mansion. From here, turn left and walk to the end of the block; turn left onto 17th Street, NW, and continue one block to Pennsylvania Avenue. The **Renwick Gallery** *(see p99)* on the corner has a magnificent exterior and houses fascinating exhibits. Continuing east on Pennsylvania Avenue, you can view the renowned north portico of the **White House** *(see pp16–19)* on your right. Reverse direction, return to 17th Street, and turn left to take in the ornate **Eisenhower Executive Office Building** *(see p49)*. A block south stands the Corcoran School of the Arts and Design, whose galleries will reopen in 2018. Admire its wonderful Beaux Arts atrium and grab a bite to eat at the nearby **Taylor Gourmet** *(see p103)*.

AFTERNOON

After leaving the Corcoran, turn right and continue down 17th Street one block to D Street. Turn right, and almost at the end of the block you'll see the entrance of the **Daughters of the American Revolution**. In addition to its fascinating period rooms, its gift shop is a treat for anyone with an interest in historic reproductions or porcelain. End your day by hailing a taxi on 17th Street to the **Kennedy Center** *(see p99)* and enjoy dinner at the **Roof Terrace Restaurant** *(see p103)*, which offers diners breathtaking views of the Potomac River.

See map on pp98–9

Political Scandals

1 Benedict Arnold

During in the early years of the American Revolution, Arnold was a military leader on the Colonists' side. But driven by money, he conspired to turn over to the British the army installation at West Point, of which he was then in command. When the plot was uncovered, he fled and then joined the British forces. His name became synonymous with "traitor."

Benedict Arnold

2 Thomas Jefferson and Sally Hemings

The press commented in the early 1800s that Jefferson had had an affair and borne children with his slave, Sally Hemings. Jefferson denied the accusations, but DNA evidence makes the link probable.

3 Andrew Jackson and the Petticoat Affair

Margaret Eaton, wife of President Jackson's secretary of war, was rumored to have had a scandalous past. Jackson defended her honor and his enemies attacked, threatening his presidency.

4 "Boss" Shepherd

Alexander Shepherd pushed the Board of Public Works to great accomplishments in the 1870s, but he was later run out of town for bankrupting city government.

5 Whiskey Ring

In 1875, it was revealed that liquor taxes were being evaded by distillers and the officials they bribed. There were 110 convictions. President Grant secured the acquittal of his private secretary.

6 Teapot Dome

The oil fields at Teapot Dome, Wyoming, had been set aside as a reserve for the US Navy. In the 1920s, oil interests bribed government officials to lease the land to them, without competitive bidding.

7 Watergate

In 1972, President Nixon's re-election workers broke into the Democrats' Watergate offices to gather campaign information. When exposed by the *Washington Post*, the conspiracy, and President Nixon's involvement in the scandal, forced him to resign in 1974.

Watergate Committee members

8 Wilbur Mills and Fanne Foxe

Wilbur Mills, chairman of the powerful House Ways and Means Committee, was caught frolicking with his friend, stripper Fanne Foxe. He was forced to resign in 1974.

9 Iran-Contra Affair

In the 1980s, Ronald Reagan's administration carried out plans to secretly sell US weapons to Iran and use the proceeds to support Nicaraguan rebels. The investigation revealed deception and corruption.

10 Bill Clinton and Monica Lewinsky

Clinton's denial of sexual relations with the White House intern led to charges of perjury, obstruction of justice, and an investigation by the House of Representatives.

Places to Eat

PRICE CATEGORIES
For a three-course meal for one with half
a bottle of wine (or equivalent meal),
taxes and extra charges.

$ under $50 $$ $50–100 $$$ over $100

1 Blue Duck Tavern
MAP M3 ▪ 1201 24th St, NW
▪ 202-419-6755 ▪ $$

The chef's specialties are prepared
before your eyes in an open kitchen
at this restaurant. Must-try dishes
include thick fries cooked in duck
fat, and mini apple pies.

2 Founding Farmers
MAP N3 ▪ 1924 Pennsylvania
Ave, NW ▪ 202-822-8783 ▪ $$

Both sustainable and stylish, this
celebration of fresh food is brought
to you by a collective of American
family farmers.

3 Equinox
MAP N3 ▪ 818 Connecticut
Ave, NW ▪ 202-331-8118 ▪ $$

A showplace for fresh local produce,
Equinox also boasts a chef, Todd
Gray, who is a pioneer in modern
American cooking. The menu is sea-
sonal and features many organic,
sustainable ingredients.

Interior of Equinox

4 Georgia Brown's
MAP P3 ▪ 950 15th St, NW
▪ 202-393-4499 ▪ $$

Southern cooking with very generous
portions of both food and attention.
Chicken, fish, stews, corn bread,
shrimp, and grits highlight the menu.

5 Marcel's
MAP M3 ▪ 2401 Pennsylvania
Ave, NW ▪ 202-296-1166 ▪ $$$

Award-winning French and Belgian
cuisine, including crispy skate wing
and Carolina pheasant, wins rave
reviews. There is a pre-theater
menu available for $85.

6 Circle Bistro
MAP M3 ▪ 1 Washington Circle,
NW ▪ 202-293-5390 ▪ $$

Circle Bistro is close to the Kennedy
Center and is a great spot for pre-
theater dinner and drinks.

7 La Perla
MAP M3 ▪ 2600 Pennsylvania
Ave, NW ▪ 202-333-1767 ▪ $$

Traditional Italian fare with a focus
on pasta, seafood, wine, and des-
serts is on offer at La Perla.

8 Roof Terrace Restaurant
MAP M4 ▪ 2700 F St, NW ▪ 202-
416-8555 ▪ $$

LOcated at the Kennedy Center (see
p99), this elegant restaurant offers
diners unrivaled views over the
Potomac River.

9 Prime Rib
MAP N3 ▪ 2020 K St, NW ▪
202-466-8811 ▪ Closed Sun ▪ $$$

Steaks and chops dominate, also
seafood and a vegetable platter.
Jacket required for men.

10 Taylor Gourmet
MAP N4 ▪ 1750 Pennsylvania
Ave, NW ▪ Open 11am–7pm Mon–Fri
& 11am–3pm Sat & Sun ▪ $

Close to the White House, this hip
version of a local deli chain makes
the best sandwiches around.

See map on pp98–9

ⓉⓄⓅ10 Georgetown

When Abigail Adams arrived in the city in 1800, she described Georgetown as "the very dirtiest hole I ever saw." It was then a major port with a huge slave and tobacco trade, cheap housing, and commercial wharves. But the Chesapeake and Ohio Canal and the Baltimore and Ohio Railroad brought prosperity to Georgetown, and therefore style. When the canal began to fail, the district went with it, until Franklin D. Roosevelt partly rehabilitated the area. Its current modish status dates back to the Kennedy era, when Georgetown became fashionable.

Fountain in Dumbarton Oaks

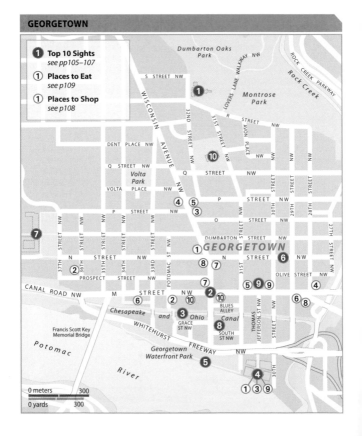

GEORGETOWN

1 Top 10 Sights
see pp105–107

1 Places to Eat
see p109

1 Places to Shop
see p108

0 meters 300
0 yards 300

1 Dumbarton Oaks Museum and Gardens

MAP L1 ■ 1703 32nd St, NW ■ 202-339-6401 ■ Museum open 11:30am–5:30pm Tue–Sun; gardens open Mar–Oct: 2–6pm Tue–Sun ■ Adm

This elegant Federal-style house, with its Philip Johnson-designed wing, houses a world-renowned collection of Byzantine and pre-Columbian artifacts. El Greco's *Visitation* is here also, possibly the Spanish master's last painting. The house and its museum are enclosed by acres of delightful landscaping, including a charming rose garden, a sparkling fountain terrace, and an orangery. In spring, this is one of the loveliest and most peaceful spots in the city to see cherry trees in blossom *(see p49)*.

2 M Street and Wisconsin Avenue

MAP L2

This intersection is surrounded by the main shopping, entertainment, dining, and bar-crawling areas of Georgetown. The attractive shops include retailers of cool urban clothes, jewelry, fine wine, gourmet foods, art and antiques, and other specialties. Restaurant food of every description is available, from modern gourmet to casual eateries.

3 Chesapeake and Ohio Canal

MAP L3 ■ Visitor Center: 1057 Thomas Jefferson St, NW; 202-653-5190; open 9am–4:30pm Wed–Sun; closed winter

The C&O Canal grew from a dream of George Washington's as a gateway to commerce in the "west" ("west" meaning Ohio at the time). Coal, flour, fur, timber, whiskey, iron ore, and other goods traveled on barges, towed by mules walking along canal-side paths. The canal's commercial days are over, but its entire length from Georgetown to Maryland has been turned into one of the most beloved National Parks in the region. You can experience the beauty and serenity of the canal by walking about a block south from M Street,

Chesapeake and Ohio Canal

NW, and turning west onto the canal's towpath. Then walk the lovely 1.5-mile (2.5-km) stretch to Abner Cloud House, where you can rent bicycles. The National Park Service Visitor Center for the C&O Canal offers plenty of useful guidance for enjoying the canal and its sur-roundings. Guided tours are also available *(see p60)*.

4 Washington Harbour

MAP L3 ■ 3000–20 K St, NW, at the bottom of Thomas Jefferson St, NW (between 30th & 31st Sts)

Good restaurants and dockside cafés; the Watergate complex and the Thompson boathouse; lovely views of the Potomac River and the Kennedy Center; walkways for strolling and benches for resting – all of these attractions and more make the harbor a magnet for Georgetowners. As a bonus, in win-ter the fountain area transforms into DC's largest outdoor skating rink. On the west side, a riverfront walkway leads to the lush green paths and tree shaded benches of Georgetown Waterfront Park *(see p106)*.

Washington Harbour

5 Georgetown Waterfront Park

MAP L3 ■ Water St, NW ■ www.georgetownwaterfrontpark.org

This park runs along the Potomac between Washington Harbour and Key Bridge. A large, interactive fountain delights and dampens children on hot days and broad stone steps lead down to the water's edge.

6 N Street

MAP L2

Little attractions and oddities abound on this street, which is noted for its exemplary architecture. Best seen from the sidewalk on 28th Street, NW, the house at No. 2726 has an outstanding mosaic by Marc Chagall, a friend of the former owner. The elegant Federal house at No. 3038 was home to Ambassador Averell Harriman, who lent the house to Jacqueline Kennedy after her husband's assassination. She later bought the elaborate 1794 Thomas Beall House across the street. Lessons in 19th-century architecture can be learned from the Federal houses at Nos. 3327 and 3339, the Second-Empire home at No. 3025–7, and the Victorian homes of Wheatley Row at Nos. 3041–45.

A row of houses on N Street

7 Georgetown University

MAP K2 ■ Room 103, White-Gravenor Hall, O & 37th Sts, NW ■ 202-687-5084 ■ Call for opening hours

This venerable institution sits on its hill overlooking Georgetown and the Potomac like a medieval citadel, its

Georgetown University

stone towers seemingly brooding with age. Yet the university is one of the most progressive in the country. Among the many interesting buildings here is the 1875 Healy Hall, built in an elaborate Flemish Renaissance style with surprising spiral adornment. Visitors can obtain campus maps and suggestions for strolls at Room 103, White-Gravenor Hall.

8 Grace Church

MAP L3 ■ 1041 Wisconsin Ave, NW (one block south of M St) ■ Open by appt (tel: 202-333-7100); office open 10am–6pm Mon, Tue, & Fri

This 1866 church was built to house a congregation founded to serve the boatmen and support staff of the

---

RIDE THE CIRCULATOR TO GEORGETOWN

Since Georgetown has no Metrorail station, it used to be difficult for visitors to get to the area's attractions. The big red buses of the DC Circulator now alleviate the problem, running daily every 10 minutes on two routes that provide cheap access to Georgetown. The first route connects Dupont Circle (19th and N Streets), Georgetown, and Rosslyn Metro station. The second route runs from Union Station to downtown Georgetown. Circulator buses run between 7am and midnight and cost $1 (see p119).

A MORNING IN GEORGETOWN

Begin at **Washington Harbour** (see p105) for its views of the Potomac River right from the waterfront. Take a pleasant stroll along the river before heading up Thomas Jefferson Street, NW, to the National Park Service Visitor Center for the **Chesapeake and Ohio Canal** (see p105). Then turn right and continue up Thomas Jefferson Street for a short block and cross M Street, NW. In front of you is the **Old Stone House**. National Park Service interpreters recreate some of the daily activities that might have taken place in this lovely old house in the 18th century.

Reverse direction and return down Thomas Jefferson Street to the canal. Turn right onto the towpath and stroll two blocks until you reach an opening in the embankment. Follow the steps to the right to Wisconsin Avenue, NW. Cross the street to lovely little **Grace Church**, built for the spiritual needs of workers on the canal. The grounds, with their mature trees, make a peaceful relaxation spot. Recross the canal and walk up to the shops at the intersection of **M Street and Wisconsin Avenue** (see p105).

Before an afternoon of retail therapy, turn left on M Street for lunch at the popular **Clyde's of Georgetown** (see p109), whose menu uses seasonal, local produce, or try one of the many side-street cafés.

C&O Canal. The simple but very elegant design brings back the mid-19th century, although without the raucous bustle that must have accompanied the canal at its peak. The grounds are beautifully peaceful. The church offers poetry readings, theater performances, and concerts.

⑨ Old Stone House
MAP L2 ▪ 3051 M St, NW ▪ 202-426-6851 ▪ Open 11am–6pm daily ▪ www.nps.gov/olst

This remarkable residence, dating from 1765, looks a little incongruous in the heart of the shopping area, but provides a captivating window into 18th-century life. There are tours, and fascinating demonstrations of the crafts and tasks of colonial families.

⑩ Tudor Place
MAP L2 ▪ 1644 31st St, NW ▪ 202-965-0400 ▪ Tours of the house 10am–4pm Tue–Sat, noon–4pm Sun; gardens: open 10am–4pm Tue–Sat, noon–4pm Sun; closed Jan, federal holidays ▪ Adm

This house-museum is remarkable for its beauty as well as its historic interest. Completed in 1816, it was built by Thomas Peter, son of a Georgetown tobacco merchant, and Martha Custis Peter, granddaughter of Martha Washington. The Peter family lived here for six generations and hosted many prominent guests.

Red door of Grace Church

Places to Shop

① Lou Lou Boutique
MAP L2 ■ 1304 Wisconsin Ave, NW

Fashion accessories, from formal to casual, fill this trendy and personable shop. Great selection of scarves, wraps, and hats, as well as an array of bags and jewelry.

② Dean & DeLuca
MAP L2 ■ 3276 M St, NW

This gourmet food store, which originated in New York, is about as luxurious as a grocery store can get. The salad bar is superb, and the ready-made meals have brought success to countless Georgetown dinner parties.

③ Appalachian Spring
MAP L2 ■ 1415 Wisconsin Ave, NW

This shop might as well be an informal museum, considering the quality of many of the handmade crafts for sale. The jewelry, carved wood, pottery, and fabrics would grace any setting.

④ The Phoenix
MAP L2 ■ 1514 Wisconsin Ave, NW

A charming, family-run store with contemporary clothing in natural fibers, classic jewelry, folk and fine art, unique items of homeware, and Mexican antiques.

⑤ Christ Child Society Opportunity Shop
MAP L2 ■ 1427 Wisconsin Ave, NW

A treasure trove of antiques and collectibles, with proceeds going to charity. Best items upstairs.

⑥ Jeweler's Werk Galerie
MAP K3 ■ 3319 Cadys Alley, NW

A showplace of handcrafted jewelry and wearable art, tucked away in Georgetown's Cadys Alley design enclave. The store is stocked with intricate necklaces, earrings, and brooches by artists and designers.

John Fluevog Shoes

⑦ John Fluevog Shoes
MAP L2 ■ 1265 Wisconsin Ave, NW

Canadian designer John Fluevog brings his colorful, funky style and distinctive brand of unique, comfortable, and trendy shoes for women as well as men to this historic quarter.

⑧ Bridge Street Books
MAP L3 ■ 2814 Pennsylvania Ave, NW

Georgetown has few dedicated bookstores – this narrow, two-storey townhouse is fertile ground for anyone with a serious interest in history, literature, film, politics, philosophy, cultural studies, or poetry.

⑨ Hu's Shoes
MAP L3 ■ 3005 M St, NW

Visit this chic boutique for high-end women's shoes from emerging designers that you won't find in department stores.

⑩ Georgetown Tobacco
MAP L3 ■ 3144 M St, NW

A neighborhood fixture for more than 40 years, this quaint tobacco shop sells more than 100 brands of cigars, hand-sculpted pipes, and humidors.

Places to Eat

PRICE CATEGORIES
For a three-course meal for one with half a bottle of wine (or equivalent meal), taxes and extra charges.

$ under $50 **$$** $50–100 **$$$** over $100

1 Farmers Fishers Bakers
MAP L3 ▪ 3000 K St, NW ▪ 202-298-8783 ▪ $$

From the same folks that created the phenomenally popular Founding Farmers (see p103), this Washington Harbour restaurant offers ultra-fresh, agriculturally sustainable, farm-to-table cuisine, with something for everyone – juicy steaks, pizza, jambalaya, and ultra-fresh sushi and fish dishes.

2 1789
MAP K2 ▪ 1226 36th St, NW ▪ 202-965-1789 ▪ $$

Serving excellent American food, this elegant townhouse is divided into six themed rooms, and was popular with President Clinton (see p68).

3 Sequoia
MAP L3 ▪ 3000 K St, NW ▪ 202-944-4200 ▪ $$

Famous for its beautiful views of the Potomac River, this is a haven for people-watching. The modern American cuisine, emphasizing seafood, enhances the setting.

4 Das Ethiopian Cuisine
MAP L2 ▪ 1201 28th St, NW ▪ 202-333-4710 ▪ $

The large Ethiopian population in the city has produced a number of fine restaurants; this one is rated among the best. Delicious vegetarian dishes, as well as spicy meat and poultry.

5 Miss Saigon
MAP L2 ▪ 3057 M St, NW ▪ 202-333-5545 ▪ $

The vegetarian specials are popular here, as well as the Vietnamese stir-fries and curries.

6 Cafe Tu O Tu
MAP M2 ▪ 2816 Pennsylvania Ave, NW ▪ 202-298-7777 ▪ $

This charming hole-in-the-wall offers delicious Turkish-inspired sandwiches, subs, and wraps.

7 El Centro D.F.
MAP P1 ▪ 1218 Wisconsin Ave, NW ▪ 202-333-4100 ▪ $

Savour soulful takes on traditional Mexican tacos and street food.

8 Martin's Tavern
MAP L2 ▪ 1264 Wisconsin Ave, NW ▪ 202-333-7370 ▪ $

Good tavern fare, a great bar, and a legendary booth in which John F. Kennedy proposed to Jackie.

9 Fiola Mare
MAP L2 ▪ 3050 K St, NW ▪ 202-628-0065 ▪ $$$

Impeccably prepared seafood, top-notch service, and superb views over the Potomac.

10 Clyde's of Georgetown
MAP L2 ▪ 3236 M St, NW ▪ 202-333-9180 ▪ $$

This long-time Georgetown favorite incorporates seasonal and local produce into its special menu items.

Clyde's of Georgetown

See map on p104

ᴛᴏᴘ⑩ Beyond the City Center

Mount Vernon greenhouse

Washington's monumental core is so rich in sights that visitors may be tempted to look no farther. But many delights lie within easy reach of the city center. The U Street NW corridor is a historic town center for the African-American community; Bethesda is full of fine restaurants; the Southwest waterfront is busy with commercial fishing activity; while Old Town Alexandria has a beautifully restored downtown. In complete contrast, there's the chance to experience the wilder side of the stately Potomac River at Great Falls.

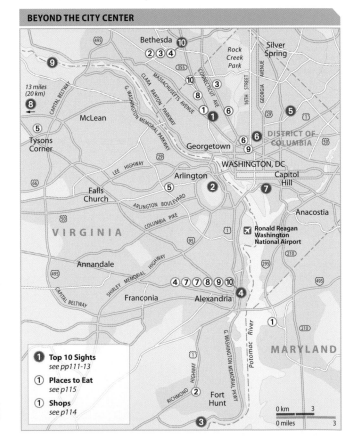

BEYOND THE CITY CENTER

① Top 10 Sights
see pp111–13

① Places to Eat
see p115

① Shops
see p114

Basilica of the National Shrine of the Immaculate Conception

1 Washington National Cathedral

This noble church, completed in 1990, is a triumph of the English Gothic style, handcrafted using authentic methods (see pp30–31).

2 Arlington Cemetery

A visit to this solemn burial ground brings conflicting emotions – pride in the defenders of freedom, pleasure in the presence of its great beauty, but dismay at the loss of so many lives marked by the arrays of headstones (see pp34–5).

3 Mount Vernon

Without a doubt the finest current view of George Washington the man, and of the agrarian plantation life that was an important stream leading to the revolutionary break with Britain (see pp36–9).

4 Old Town Alexandria
MAP D5

This lovely old city center, across the Potomac just beneath the capital, retains the charm and hospitality of its illustrious past while giving visitors all modern conveniences, including a metro station (King Street on the yellow and blue lines). Alexandria is noted for its historical and archeological museums, Gadsby's Tavern (see p48), the evocative system of Civil War forts and defenses at Fort Ward, and its captivating residential architecture, civilized shops, and restaurants.

5 Basilica of the National Shrine of the Immaculate Conception
MAP D3 ▪ 400 Michigan Ave, NE ▪ 202-526-8300 ▪ Open Nov–Mar: 7am–6pm daily; Apr–Oct: 7am–7pm daily

This mammoth basilica, dedicated in 1959, incorporates more than 60 chapels and oratories that retell the diverse history of the Roman Catholic Church in the United States. Conceived in the grand style – it is the largest Roman Catholic church in the Western hemisphere – the building combines Byzantine and Romanesque features, creating an intensely decorative but substantial effect. The interior is overwhelming in its grandeur, whatever your faith. There is also an on-site cafeteria serving breakfast and lunch, which is convenient because there are few nearby restaurants. Free docent-led tours are available.

Old Town Alexandria

6 U Street, NW
MAP N1

For much of the 20th century, U Street, NW, was the main street of this bustling and prosperous African-American neighborhood. Opened as a movie theater in 1922, the Lincoln Theatre *(see p67)* has now been refurbished and presents performances of every kind. Next door is the famous Ben's Chili Bowl, turning out great simple food for capacity crowds. The legendary jazz musician Duke Ellington *(see p47)* played his first paid performance at True Reformer Hall at the junction of 12th and U Street, NW. The poignant sculpture and plaza of the African-American Civil War Memorial *(see p51)* commemorates African-Americans who served their country in the Civil War.

Ben's Chili Bowl shop sign

> **NATIONAL CATHEDRAL SCHOOLS**
>
> Like a medieval cathedral, National Cathedral is surrounded by some of the most prestigious prep schools in the city. St. Albans' alumni include Al Gore and Jesse Jackson, Jr. The all-girls National Cathedral School is alma mater to a number of Rockefellers and Roosevelts. Sidwell Friends School, just along Wisconsin Avenue, educated Chelsea Clinton, the Nixon daughters, Nancy Davis Reagan, and Barack Obama's daughters.

three new hotels and an array of unique stores fill the area, and there is live music at the Anthem and Pearl Street Warehouse. The entire area is being upgraded with parks and green spaces.

7 Southwest Waterfront
MAP D4 ■ Water St, SW

This is a wonderful place for a stroll, summer and winter. The diversity of Washington is on parade, the sailboats, yachts, and houseboats are picturesque, and the seafood – both cooked and raw – is a showcase of what's best in eastern waters. The Wharf has transformed the waterfront into a modern destination. Over a dozen restaurants – from casual dining to upscale seafood – plus

8 National Air and Space Museum Steven F. Udvar-Hazy Center

This display and restoration center for some of the museum's magnificent collection of historic aviation and space artifacts *(see pp20–21)* opened in December 2003 near Dulles International Airport. Two giant hangars with accompanying support buildings, sprawled across 17 acres (7 ha), feature thousands of artifacts, including the space shuttle *Discovery*, a Concorde, and a Lockheed SR-71 Blackbird.

National Air and Space Museum Steven F. Udvar-Hazy Center

9 Great Falls
MAP A2 ■ Falls open dawn–dusk daily ■ Great Falls Tavern Visitor Center: 11710 MacArthur Blvd; 310-767-3714; www.nps.gov/choh

About 15 miles (24 km) north of Washington, DC, the Potomac is rent by magnificent waterfalls over the crags and sluices of the eroded river bed. In the state of Virginia, Great Falls Park is reached from Old Dominion Drive (Route 738). It provides spectacular overlooks above the river, hiking trails, and the ruins of a small 19th-century town. On the Maryland side, the Great Falls area is part of the C&O Canal (see p105). The Great Falls Tavern Visitor Center offers canal boat rides, hiking, and ranger-led tours, and there are remarkable river views from the overlook on Olmstead Island.

Whitewater rapids at Great Falls

10 Bethesda, Maryland
MAP C2

Locally, Bethesda is best known for its enormous quantity and range of restaurants, most of them clustered into a lively downtown area that still retains the charming atmosphere of a traditional town center. The high-end professional employment offered by Bethesda's world-renowned bio-technology industry has also generated a spirited music, performance, and arts scene that caters to its cultured and wealthy residents. The city is especially strong on public art. Its streets and parks spotlight distinguished contemporary works in every style, by way of sculpture and stunning painted murals.

A DAY IN OLD TOWN ALEXANDRIA

MORNING

Begin at **Christ Church** (118 N Washington St; open 9am–4pm Mon–Sat, 2–4pm Sun; donation), a handsome Georgian-style building completed in 1773. George Washington's box pew has been preserved. Then turn right onto Cameron Street toward the harbor. Continue three blocks and turn right onto North Royal Street. The two buildings on your right comprise **Gadsby's Tavern Museum** (see p48). The tours involve an introduction to colonial life in the city. Continue one block and turn left onto King Street. On Saturday morning, it hosts a historic Farmers Market. Continue south to the **Stabler-Leadbeater Apothecary Museum** (107 S Fairfax St; open Apr–Oct: 10am–5pm Tue–Sat, 1–5pm Sun; Nov–Mar: 11am–4pm Wed–Sat, 1pm–4pm Sun; adm). Here you will find herbal botanicals, handblown glass, and medical equipment from the 1800s.

AFTERNOON

Enjoy lunch or a snack at one of the many restaurants along King Street, then continue toward the harbor to North Union Street, and turn left to shop for original artwork at the popular **Torpedo Factory Art Center** (see p114), home to more than 80 working artist studios open to the public, plus seven galleries and the EatsPlace Café and Market, which serves light fare. Directly behind the art center is the **Potomac Riverboat Company** (potomacriverboatco.com), which runs cruises to Mount Vernon and around Alexandria Seaport.

See map on p110

Shops

1 National Harbor
MAP D6 ▪ 165 Waterfront St, National Harbor, MD 20745

Seventy shops line the streets of this trendy neighborhood. Designer jewelry and fashion are prominent, as are specialty shops selling fine foods, wines, and even motorcycles. Nearby Tanger offers another 85 brand-name outlets.

2 Mount Vernon Antique Center
MAP C6 ▪ 8101 Richmond Hwy, Alexandria, VA 22309

This is one of the area's oldest and best-known antiques malls, with over 30 independent dealers selling a vast array of items. The very popular Modern Montage offers mid-20th-century furniture and kitsch.

3 Politics and Prose
MAP H2 ▪ 5015 Connecticut Ave, NW

A bookstore with a large selection of works on politics, culture, and government. A cheerful place, despite its serious stock, with a café.

4 Fibre Space
MAP C5 ▪ 1319 King St, Alexandria, VA 22314

This Old Town Alexandria shop is filled with a dazzling assortment of colorful yarns from local, sustainable sources. Knitting equipment can be found here as well: needles, crochet hooks, patterns, and more.

5 Tysons Corner Center and Tysons Galleria
Buses run from Ballston Metro to this huge shopping site, with stores catering to every budget as well as cinemas and restaurants *(see p69)*.

6 Kramerbooks
MAP N2 ▪ 1517 Connecticut Ave, NW

This Dupont Circle landmark has a fantastic collection of books and knowledgeable staff. There's also

Afterwords Café at Kramerbooks

a bar and restaurant, the Afterwords Café. The store is open until 3am on Fridays and Saturdays.

7 Torpedo Factory Art Center
MAP D5 ▪ 105 N Union St, Alexandria

Originally a torpedo-making factory, today the site contains 82 studios and seven galleries where artists and craftspeople create work and offer it for sale. Prints, ceramics, photography, painting, and sculpture.

8 Sullivan's Toy Store
MAP G4 ▪ 4200 Wisconsin Ave, NW

An astounding range of playthings can be found in this store, but the real stars are the items with a link to the past: model kits, craft supplies, board games, and kites.

9 Chocolate Moose
MAP N3 ▪ 1743 L St NW ▪ 202-463-0992

This shop located between the White House and Dupont Circle specializes in the weird and wonderful. You will find confections, housewares, tacky toys and much more.

10 Kron Chocolatier
MAP G2 ▪ Mazza Galleria, 5300 Wisconsin Ave, NW

This store is famous for its molded chocolate items – bears, sports cars, even the US Capitol. They also sell greeting cards made of chocolate.

Places to Eat

PRICE CATEGORIES
For a three-course meal for one with half a bottle of wine (or equivalent meal), taxes and extra charges.

$ under $50 $$ $50–100 $$$ over $100

1 Two Amys
MAP H4 ▪ 3715 Macomb St, NW ▪ 202-885-5700 ▪ $

Within easy walking distance of the National Cathedral, this is the favorite pizzeria of the locals – expect to wait for a table during peak times. Authentic Neapolitan pizzas baked in a wood-burning oven.

2 American Tap Room
MAP C2 ▪ 7278 Woodmont Ave, Bethesda, MD ▪ 301-656-1366 ▪ $

A modern version of the traditional American tap room, this offers an inviting atmosphere, large selection of beers, and classic grill menu. Open for brunch, lunch, and dinner.

3 Bacchus of Lebanon
MAP C2 ▪ 7945 Norfolk Ave, Bethesda, MD ▪ 301-657-1722 ▪ $$

Don't miss the delicious meze at this Lebanese restaurant. Marinated chicken, roast eggplant (aubergine), hummus, and squid fill numerous little dishes with flavor.

4 Passage to India
MAP C2 ▪ 4931 Cordell Ave, Bethesda, MD ▪ 301-656-3373 ▪ $

The menu here does not limit itself to any particular region of India. The dal (lentils) and butter chicken are rich and smooth.

5 Grand Cru
MAP C4 ▪ 4301 Wilson Blvd, Arlington, VA ▪ 703-243-7900 ▪ $$

This tiny café has an exquisite menu, including succulent filet mignon and moreish crème brûlée. Doubling as a wine shop, it has an outstanding selection available. Dine in the courtyard in good weather.

6 Ardeo+Bardeo
MAP H4 ▪ 3311 Connecticut Ave, NW ▪ 202-244-6750 ▪ $$

This is a hip bistro/bar delivering new American cuisine. Book a roof deck table in summer.

7 Bilbo Baggins Restaurant
MAP D5 ▪ 208 Queen St, Alexandria, VA ▪ 703-683-0300 ▪ $$

The menu fuses dishes from around the world and features a wonderful selection of beers.

8 Vermillion
MAP D5 ▪ 1120 King St, Alexandria, VA 22314 ▪ 703-684-9669 ▪ $$$

Consistently listed among the best restaurants in Alexandria, this serves New American cuisine featuring farm-to-table ingredients in lively versions of traditional favorites.

Interior of Restaurant Eve

9 Restaurant Eve
MAP D5 ▪ 110 S. Pitt St, Alexandria ▪ 703-706-0450 ▪ $$$

Wood and amber create a cozy ambience here. There is a cocktails and nibbles lounge, a bistro, and a tasting room. Don't miss the butter-poached Maine lobster.

10 Taverna Cretekou
MAP D5 ▪ 818 King St, Alexandria, VA ▪ 703-548-8688 ▪ $

Fantastic Greek food, ouzo, and traditional dancing can be found at this popular restaurant.

See map on p110

Streetsmart

U Street/African-Amer Civil War
Memorial/Cardozo metro station

Getting To and Around Washington, DC

Arriving by Air

The city is served by three major airports. Most international flights arrive at **Dulles International (IAD)** 26 miles (42 km) west of the city. **Baltimore-Washington International (BWI)** is 30 miles (48 km) northeast of DC. **Reagan National (DCA)** is located just 5 miles (8 km) from the city center.

Transportation from each of the airports into the city center can be accessed direct from the baggage claim area.

From Dulles airport the **Washington Flyer** Silver Line Express Bus goes to the Wiehle-Reston East Metrorail Station for transit on the Metrorail. **SuperShuttle** shared vans provide a service throughout the area, or you can take a cab or Uber.

From BWI, there is train service on the **Maryland Rail Commuter Service (MARC)** and Amtrak. There is an express Metrobus service to Greenbelt Metrorail Station. SuperShuttle and taxis are also available.

Reagan National offers Metrorail, SuperShuttle, and taxi services.

Arriving by Train

Amtrak provides intercity rail transport, stopping at Union Station. For travel between DC and Boston, Acela Express is the quickest way to reach New York and other major East Coast cities. Amtrak has a reduced-fare USA Rail Pass, which is worth considering if traveling widely across the country.

Arriving by Car

Washington streets are congested most of the time, and often gridlocked at rush hour (6:30am–9:30am and 4–7pm). There is limited parking available near the attractions, making driving a less attractive option than public transportation. Some of the larger hotels have parking, and public lots are available. Driving routes to DC are I-95 and I-270 from the north, I-66 from the west, I-95 and I-395 from the south, and US 50 from the east. I-95 and I-495 form a heavily used interstate beltway around Washington, DC.

Arriving by Bus

The main bus terminals are behind Union Station, with some lines stopping just across the street. **Greyhound** connects with over 3,700 locations, and offers budget passes. Other bus companies include **BestBus, Bolt Bus**, and **Megabus**.

Traveling by Metrorail

For most destinations in the city, **Metrorail**, the subway-surface rail system, is the best way to get around. Service is frequent, cars are clean and comfortable, stops are convenient for major sights, and the system is among the safest in the world. Fares depend on the time of day and distance traveled, ranging from $2.25 to $6. There are one-day, seven-day, and 28-day passes that allow unlimited trips for a reduced fare. Stations are marked with a large "M," and system maps and fares are posted on the mezzanine level where the station manager is usually available to answer questions.

Traveling by Metrobus and the DC Circulator

The public **Metrobus** system serves all areas of the city. Exact change is required (regular routes are $1.75). **DC Circulator** buses travel six useful routes every ten minutes. Exact change is required ($1.00 fare).

It is well worth buying a SmarTrip fare card at any Metrorail station for convenience and discounts on the Metrorail, Metrobus, Circulator, and other regional transit systems, as well as for free bus-to-bus transfers.

Traveling by Car

Driving is undoubtedly the least efficient way to get around in the core DC area. There are few gas stations and a lot of one-way streets and time-of-day parking restrictions. The streets are laid out in a grid; the north–south streets are numbered, while the east–west streets are named with letters. Diagonal streets are named after states and cross the grid in both directions. Addresses contain NE, SE, SW, or NW indicating their position relative to the Capitol building which is at the center of the grid.

Parking in a lot will cost you about $20 per day or about $12 for two hours. Street parking meters have a two-hour maximum stay, and fines are high. Parking is prohibited on a great many downtown streets during rush hour, with hours posted on curbside signs. Your car will be towed if you disregard them.

Zipcar rents cars by the hour or by the day. Plan members (pre-approved plus $70 membership) can reserve a car for pick up at a Metro station.

Rates start at $12.75 (gas and insurance included). **Car2Go** rents cars by the minute, hour, or day plus a one-time $5 fee.

Rental car companies, including **Avis**, **Budget**, and **Hertz**, are located at airports, Union Station, and many other locations. Renting a car requires a valid driver's license and a major credit card, and drivers must be at least 25 years old.

Traveling by Taxi

DC taxis are metered, and there are more than 100 companies from which to choose. The **GoCurb** taxi app connects you to local firms, or you can get a taxi from the **Yellow Cab Company of DC**. You'll find taxis waiting outside most hotels, too. Expect to pay a "drop" fee of $3.50, and 27 cents every one-eighth of a mile. Bulky luggage and additional passengers will be charged as extra. There is a $25/hour waiting fee. There is also **Uber**, which lets you summon a rideshare car by smartphone, billing your credit card.

Traveling by Bicycle and on Foot

Washington is a city built for walking, with wide sidewalks and courteous drivers. Busy streets have pedestrian walk lights at intersections. But the central attractions of the city are quite spread out, so pack a pair of comfortable shoes. **Capital Bikeshare** has bicycles for hire at around 440 locations. Single trip, one-day, three-day, or monthly passes are available.

DIRECTORY

ARRIVING BY AIR

Baltimore/Washington International (BWI)
🅦 bwiairport.com

Dulles International (IAD)
🅦 flydulles.com

Maryland Rail Commuter Service (MARC)
🅦 mta.maryland.gov

Reagan National (DCA)
🅦 flyreagan.com

SuperShuttle
🅦 supershuttle.com

Washington Flyer
🅦 washfly.com

ARRIVING BY TRAIN

Amtrak
📞 800-USA-RAIL/
800-872-7245
🅦 amtrak.com

ARRIVING BY BUS

BestBus
🅦 bestbus.com

Bolt Bus
🅦 boltbus.com

Greyhound
🅦 greyhound.com

Megabus
🅦 megabus.com

TRAVELING BY METRORAIL

Metrorail
📞 202-637-7000
🅦 wmata.com

TRAVELING BY METROBUS AND THE DC CIRCULATOR

DC Circulator
📞 202-962-1423
🅦 dccirculator.com

Metrobus
📞 202-637-7000
🅦 wmata.com

TRAVELING BY CAR

Avis
🅦 avis.com

Budget
🅦 budget.com

Car2Go
🅦 car2go.com

Hertz
🅦 hertz.com

Zipcar
🅦 zipcar.com

TRAVELING BY TAXI

GoCurb
🅦 www.gocurb.com

Uber
🅦 www.uber.com

Yellow Cab Company of DC
🅦 dcyellowcab.com

TRAVELING BY BICYCLE AND ON FOOT

Capital Bikeshare
🅦 capitalbikeshare.com

Practical Information

Passports and Visas

Canadian and Mexican visitors require valid passports to enter the US. Citizens of 38 countries, including most European nations, Australia, and New Zealand, do not need a visa, but must have a passport and apply to enter in advance via the **Electronic System for Travel Authorization (ESTA)**. All other visitors require a tourist visa and passport to enter, and will be photographed and have fingerprints checked by the **Transportation Security Administration**. Entry regulations may change, so check well in advance of travel with the US Department of State for the latest information.

Most countries have embassies here, including **Canada**, **Ireland**, and the **UK**, and can offer limited consular assistance to their nationals. There's a full list at **embassy.org**.

Customs and Immigration

Nonresident travelers to the US need to complete a **Customs and Border Protection** form, and may carry $100 in gifts; one liter of alcohol as beer, wine, or liquor (age 21 years or older); and one carton of cigarettes, 50 cigars (not Cuban), or two kilograms (4.4 lbs) smoking tobacco without incurring tax.

Travel Safety Advice

Visitors can get up-to-date travel safety information from the **UK Foreign and Commonwealth Office**, the **US Department of State**, and the **Australian Department of Foreign Affairs and Trade**.

Travel Insurance

Medical insurance is highly recommended for international travelers, as costs for medical and dental care can be very high. Insurance against trip cancellation, air travel delays, and lost baggage is also advisable. Car rental agencies offer vehicle and liability insurance, but check your policy before traveling.

Health

No vaccinations will be required for visiting the US. Pack medications in their original, labeled containers. You can carry unused syringes and injectable prescription medication. Your hotel will usually recommend a doctor if you need one. Or you can contact a service such as **Doctors To You** whose members will come to your room.

MedStar Georgetown University Hospital has a free weekday physician referral service, while **Children's National** is one of the country's top pediatric centers. Walk-in clinics such as **Farragut Medical and Travel Care** are also available, and for minor injuries some pharmacies have nurse practitioners. For emergency dental care, contact **1-800-dentist**. The **CVS** drugstore chain has many 24-hour pharmacies, including those at Dupont Circle and Wisconsin Ave, NW, and can refer you to branches in other areas.

Personal Security

Washington is a large, cosmopolitan city and is generally safe in the tourist areas. Petty crime does exist, so be alert to your surroundings, leave your valuables and passport in a hotel safe, get a receipt for stored luggage, and be discreet with expensive jewelry, cameras, and phones. Split your cash and cards between wallets and pockets, keep wallets in inside pockets, and carry a cross-body purse. Keep copies of your documents and ID separately.

The eastern part of DC is a rapidly gentrifying area and is generally safe, but there are areas of the city where extra vigilance and care are required, especially at night. Ask your hotel concierge for advice if you are unsure.

The likelihood of stolen property being recovered is slim, but it is essential that you file a claim with the **Metropolitan Police Department (MPDC)** and retain a copy of the crime report for your insurance company at home. Within the Metro's service area, you can also ask the **Metro Transit Police** for help. Note the taxi company, bus line or metro route you use to help retrieve lost belongings. If you lose your passport or believe it to have been stolen, you will need to get in touch with your embassy immediately. Call your credit card company or bank to report lost or stolen cards or travelers' checks.

Law enforcement in DC is provided by multiple national agencies, which include blue-uniformed MPDC officers who patrol the city streets and are able to assist visitors. National Park Rangers wear gray shirts and green trousers and help visitors on park property. There are also Secret Service and Special Weapons and Tactics teams, whose job is to maintain national security and protect the president.

Emergency Services

For **ambulance**, **medical**, **police**, and fire brigade services, call the national emergency number 911 and give your location and details about the problem.

Travelers with Specific Needs

Washington, DC is one of the most accessible cities in the US, but there are challenges involved with some historic buildings. Metrorail stations are accessible, with wide fare gates and elevators. Rail cars have gap reducers, emergency intercoms, and priority seating. All

Metrobuses can "kneel", and have lifts or ramps. Visitors with specific needs can apply for a Reduced Fare SmarTrip ID card. The **Metro** website also offers videos and downloadable guides. Government buildings, museums and theaters are accessible, but verify that tours can meet your requirements. It is best to call hotels and restaurants ahead of time and ask about the amenities available. Both **Reagan National Airport** and **Dulles International Airport** have accessibility guides, as does the city's official tourism site, **Destination DC**.

DIRECTORY

PASSPORTS AND VISAS

Canada
MAP Q4 ■ 501 Pennsylvania Ave, NW
w washington.gc.ca

Electronic System for Travel Authorization (ESTA)
w esta.cbp.dhs.gov/esta

embassy.org
w embassy.org

Ireland
MAP J6 ■ 2234 Massachusetts Ave, NW
w dfa.ie/irish-embassy/usa

Transportation Security Administration
w tsa.gov/travel

UK
MAP H5 ■ 3500 Massachusetts Ave, NW
w ukinusa.fco.gov.uk

CUSTOMS AND IMMIGRATION

Customs and Border Protection
Visa Waiver Program, Customs information
w cbp.gov/travel

TRAVEL SAFETY ADVICE

Australian Department of Foreign Affairs and Trade
w dfat.gov.au
w smartraveller.gov.au

UK Foreign and Commonwealth Office
w gov.uk/foreign-travel-advice

US Department of State
w travel.state.gov

HEALTH

Children's National
w childrensnational.org

CVS
MAP N2 ■ 6 Dupont Cir
☎ 202-785-1466
MAP G3 ■ 4555 Wisconsin Ave, NW
☎ 202-537-1587
w cvs.com

1-800-dentist
w 1800dentist.com

Doctors To You
☎ 202-545-3300

Farragut Medical and Travel Care
w farragutmedical.com

MedStar Georgetown University Hospital
w medstargeorgetown.org

PERSONAL SECURITY

Metropolitan Police Department (MPDC)
☎ 311 or 202-737-4404

Metro Transit Police
☎ 202-962-2121

EMERGENCY SERVICES

Ambulance, Medical, Police, and Fire Brigade
☎ 911

TRAVELERS WITH SPECIFIC NEEDS

Destination DC
w washington.org

Dulles International Airport
w flydulles.com/iad/disability-services

Metro
w wmata.com/accessibility/

Reagan National Airport
w flyreagan.com/dca/services-patrons-disabilities

Currency and Banking

The US currency is the dollar ($), made up of 100 cents. The most common denominations of bills are $1, $5, $10, and $20, with larger denominations also available. Cents come in 1 (penny), 5 (nickel), 10 (dime), and 25 (quarter) cent coins.

It is best to convert a small amount of currency at the airport to cover immediate expenses, then later convert larger amounts at a bank from the teller or the ATM machine, using a debit card, for a better rate. Cirrus, Plus, and NCYE are the more common networks. For safety, use an ATM inside a bank. Bank ATM machines also accept credit cards, but interest will be charged. Currency bureaus such as **Travelex** and **ICE** (International Currency Exchange) are to be found at airports, Union Station, and in other key locations.

A major credit card will be needed for car rentals, hotels, and restaurants. Most services will accept Visa, Mastercard, and American Express. Cash is often required by street vendors, on buses, and for some services.

Telephone and Internet

All telephone numbers in the United States are ten digits long. The first three of these are the area code, which is 202 for Washington, DC, 703 for nearby Virginia and 240, 301, or 410 for Maryland. Dial the area code first, followed by the seven-digit phone number. Dial 0 for the operator, and 411 for directory assistance (fee). To make a direct overseas call, dial 011, the country code, city area code, and number. For an operator-assisted call, dial 01, country code, city area code, and number.

Public telephones can be found in airports and train stations, but not in many other places. It is most convenient to use a cell phone as hotels add a substantial service fee to calls made from your room. Before traveling, check with your phone carrier about service in the United States. You can rent a phone from **Cellhire**, **Cellular Abroad**, and others for overseas and US calls, or buy a disposable phone at convenience stores, office supply stores, or phone outlet stores.

Most hotels offer free Wi-Fi, but some may charge for this service. Free Wi-Fi is available at many coffee shops, libraries, several of the Smithsonian Museums and the National Gallery of Art on the Mall. Free Wi-Fi locations are listed on **Wi-Fi Free Spot** and the government website **DC Wi-Fi Hotspots**.

Postal Services

Many hotels sell stamps and will mail your letters. A standard (1 oz/28 g) letter costs 49 cents to a US destination, or $1.15 outside the US. Flat rate envelopes and boxes are available at **US Postal Service** post offices (9am to 5pm Monday to Friday) for both domestic and overseas destinations.

Television and Radio

The major television networks in the region include **CBS** (channel 9), **NBC** (channel 4), and **ABC** (channel 7). Many others are available through cable TV, which is provided by most hotels.

Radio station **WTOP** (103.5 FM) is an all-news and weather station, and **WAMU** (88.5 FM) is a member of NPR (National Public Radio).

Newspapers and Magazines

The internationally respected *Washington Post* newspaper covers local news, politics, and entertainment, as well as national and international news. Its pull-out Friday Weekend section and Going Out Guide cover Washington entertainment and events. The *Wall Street Journal* and the *New York Times* newspapers are also widely available. The monthly *Washingtonian* magazine has a good local events calendar.

Opening Hours

Office hours are usually 9am to 5pm. Stores open at 9 or 10am and close around 5 or 6pm Monday to Saturday. Some stores remain open later, and Sunday store hours vary. Grocery stores generally open 8am to 9pm daily, or longer. Some larger stores are open 24 hours. Pharmacy hours vary, from 8am to 6pm or later, and some have 24-hour service. Most banks are open 9am to 5pm Monday to Friday, and some also open Saturday morning. Most museums are open from 10am to 5:30pm, but check as times and dates can vary. Metrorail trains start at 5am Monday to Friday, 7am Saturday, and 8am on Sunday, and stop at 11:30pm from Monday to Thursday, 1am Friday and Saturday, and 11pm Sunday. Public holiday hours may be different, so check ahead of time.

Time Difference

Washington, DC is on Eastern Standard Time (EST), and is three hours ahead of California and five hours behind London. Daylight Saving Time starts at 2am on the second Sunday in March and ends at 2am on the first Sunday in November.

Electrical Appliances

The standard US electric current is 110 volts and 60 Hz current. American plugs have two flat pins; an adapter will be needed for European appliances.

Driving

Foreign visitors with a valid license from most countries are permitted to drive personal or rental cars while in the United States, but it is advisable to carry an International Driving Permit (IDP) if you plan on renting a car or driving, especially if the license is not in English, does not have a photo, or is not from a qualifying country. An IDP must be obtained in advance of your trip in the country that originally issued the driver's license.

Weather

The average DC daytime temperature ranges from a high of 89° F (32° C) in July to a low of 42° F (6° C) in January; the average nighttime temperature goes from a high of 72° F (22° C) in July to a low of 26° F (-3° C) in January. However, temperatures in every season vary greatly. Humidity can be an issue in summer, so always carry some water with you when out and about. Precipitation averages range from a high of 4 in (10 cm) in August to a low of 3 in (7 cm) in January when much of it falls as snow. Winters can be very windy and raw, with snow and ice storms that can paralyze the city.

Visitor Information

The DC **Chamber of Commerce** provides information for visitors on their website and by mail. The site has search capabilities for hotels, shops, restaurants, transportation, and tourist sights.

Destination DC *(see p121)*, Washington's official tourism site, provides information on the city's history, attractions, dining, accommodation, tours, and events, and offers useful interactive maps. Assistance is also available by phone and at their office on 7th Street, NW.

DC.Gov, the official government web portal, has an online resource center packed with useful information and links. The **Capitol Visitor Center** and the nonprofit **Cultural Tourism DC** are also excellent sources of visitor information.

DIRECTORY

CURRENCY AND BANKING

ICE
w iceplc.com

Travelex
w travelex.com

TELEPHONE AND INTERNET

Cellhire
w cellhire.com

Cellular Abroad
w cellularabroad.com

DC Wi-Fi Hotspots
w wifi.dc.gov

Wi-Fi Free Spot
w wififreespot.com

POSTAL SERVICES

US Postal Service
w usps.com

TELEVISION AND RADIO

ABC
w abc.go.com

CBS
w cbs.com

NBC
w nbc.com

WAMU
w wamu.org

WTOP
w wtop.com

NEWSPAPERS AND MAGAZINES

New York Times
w nytimes.com

Wall Street Journal
w wsj.com

Washingtonian
w washingtonian.com

Washington Post
w washingtonpost.com

VISITOR INFORMATION

Capitol Visitor Center
w visitthecapitol.gov

Chamber of Commerce
w dcchamber.org

Cultural Tourism DC
w culturaltourismdc.org

DC.Gov
w dc.gov

Trips and Tours

Bus tours are one of the most popular sightseeing options, and several bus tour companies feature double-decker vehicles with open-topped upper decks that allow great views. **Old Town Trolley Tours** run loops taking in the main sights. Riders can hop on and off, and one- or two-day passes are available. **Big Bus Tours** and **CitySights DC** also offer similar tours.

The city's abundance of sidewalks and green spaces make walking tours one of the best ways to see specific areas like the Mall, Capitol Hill, and Georgetown. Guided or self-guided tours usually last between one and three hours and can cover a lot of ground, so dress for changeable weather, carry water, and wear comfortable shoes. Try the **Spies of Washington Tour**, **Washington Walks**, or **Free Tours by Foot**.

Bicycle tours are also popular, covering long distances faster than is possible on foot, while Segway tours are a different way to explore the city. **Bike and Roll** offers both. Segway tours are also run by **Capital Segway** and **City Segway Tours**.

Potomac tours range from luxury lunch and dinner cruises with the **Potomac Riverboat Company** and **Capitol River Cruises**, where you can watch the sights of the city glide past, to thrilling land-and-water trips aboard an amphibious **DC Ducks** craft.

There is also a wide array of tours covering special interest topics, such as the food tours run by **DC Metro Food Tours**. Alternatively, you could design your own itinerary with **The Guild** of professional DC tour guides.

Shopping

Shopping is a popular activity in Washington, but it is unusual to find bargains unless it is sales season. A 6 percent sales tax is added to the purchase price. No-sales-tax days take place in August some years, before school starts, and shave extra off prices. Black Friday, the day after Thanksgiving, offers big discounts, and post-Christmas sales are also a magnet for shoppers. Promotions are common on other public holidays as well. Unique souvenirs can be found at museum shops and gift stores at other major attractions, in the form of high-quality items related to their collections, history, or special features.

Dining

The city has more than 1,000 restaurants serving almost every cuisine imaginable, with prices ranging from affordable to very expensive. Many more are available nearby in Virginia and Maryland.

Local specialties here include fresh seafood from Chesapeake Bay, and between May and September crack-your-own Chesapeake Blue Crabs are served at **The Quarterdeck**, a casual eatery on the waterfront in Arlington. Maryland crab cakes and she-crab soup are local favorites and widely available.

Locals, dignitaries, and in-the-know visitors head to **Ben's Chili Bowl** for a half-smoke, a mildly spicy chili and cheese covered smoked sausage hot dog. Farm-to-table dining at **Founding Fathers DC** offers fresh, seasonal local or regionally grown foods in a friendly, upscale setting. Its new American menu offers green salads, pot pie, sandwiches, and more. For a great take-out, head to the **Dean & Deluca** deli, which offers freshly made dishes, gourmet foods, and a great choice of fine wines.

The *Washington Post* provides a comprehensive online dining guide, and reservations at many DC restaurants can be made via **OpenTable**, which has reliable reviews.

Breakfast is generally served from 7 to 10am, lunch from 11:30am to 2pm, and dinner from 5:30 to 10pm. Food is available all day in central DC, especially at the Smithsonian Museums, Capitol Visitor Center, and the food courts at Union Station and the Ronald Reagan Building.

A 10 percent tax will be added to the dining total, and tips of 15–20 percent of the bill are expected. Alcoholic beverages are available in many restaurants. The legal age for drinking alcohol is 21, and patrons of any age may be asked for photo ID.

Accommodations

Washington offers a wide range of accommodation options. High-rise hotels, historic inns, all-suites accommodations, and trendy boutique hotels can be found near the main attractions and Metro stations. Bed-and-breakfasts, apartments, and campgrounds are usually located farther from the city center.

Prices are lowest from January through early March. Spring and summer are generally expensive, although weekend rates may be lower when Congress is not in session. Book in advance. Check on sites such as **Visit DC**, **Destination DC** (see p121), and **Hotels. com** for discount rates; **Kayak** and **Expedia** for discounted airline and hotel packages; and on hotel websites for special promotions and package deals. All rates are subject to 14.8 percent room tax, and it is usual to tip porters at least $1 for each bag, and housekeeping $1–2 a day.

In conventional hotels, some rooms may have refrigerators, microwaves, or free Wi-Fi. Suites may have a sofa bed in a living area, and often have a full kitchen.

Bed and breakfast inns are available outside the city center, and can be booked via agencies such as **Bed and Breakfast DC**. Some accept children, include a full breakfast, and offer free Wi-Fi.

Furnished apartments often provide more space and amenities at a lower price than hotels. They usually have a full kitchen but no maid service, and are often located in residential neighborhoods. Try **Vacation Rentals** and **Vacation Rentals by Owner**. Another useful option is **Airbnb**, which lists furnished apartments as well as bedrooms in private homes.

Washington has only one hostel, **Hostelling International**. There are two campgrounds located in Maryland that provide transportation service for visitors to DC, **Cherry Hill Park** and **Capitol KOA**.

DIRECTORY

TRIPS AND TOURS

Big Bus Tours
w bigbustours.com

Bike and Roll
w bikeandrolldc.com

Capital Segway
w capitalsegway.com

Capitol River Cruises
w capitolrivercruises.com

City Segway Tours
w citysegwaytours.com

CitySights DC
w citysightsdc.com

DC Ducks
w dcducks.com

DC Metro Food Tours
w dcmetrofoodtours.com

Free Tours by Foot
w freetoursbyfoot.com

The Guild
w washingtondctourguides.com

Old Town Trolley Tours
w trolleytours.com

Potomac Riverboat Company
w potomacriverboatco.com

Spies of Washington Tour
w spiesofwashingtontour.com

Washington Walks
w washingtonwalks.com

DINING

Ben's Chili Bowl
MAP P1 ■ 1213 U St, NW, Washington, DC 20009
w benschilibowl.com

Dean & Deluca
MAP L3 ■ 3276 M St, NW, Washington, DC 20007
w deandeluca.com

Founding Farmers DC
MAP N3 ■ 1924 Pennsylvania Ave, NW, Washington, DC 20006
w wearefoundingfarmers.com

OpenTable
w opentable.com

Quarterdeck
MAP K5 ■ 1200 Fort Myer Drive, Arlington, VA 22209
w quarterdeckarlington.com

Washington Post
w washingtonpost.com/goingoutguide

ACCOMMODATIONS

Airbnb
w airbnb.com

Bed and Breakfast DC
w bedandbreakfastdc.com

Capitol KOA
w koa.com

Cherry Hill Park
w cherryhillpark.com

Expedia
w expedia.com

Hostelling International
w hiwashingtondc.org

Hotels.com
w hotels.com

Kayak
w kayak.com

Vacation Rentals
w vacationrentals.com

Vacation Rentals by Owner
w vrbo.com

Visit DC
w visitdc.com

Places to Stay

PRICE CATEGORIES
For a standard, double room per night (with breakfast if included), taxes and extra charges.

$ under $200 ■ $$ $200–350 ■ $$$ over $350

Historic Hotels

Tabard Inn
MAP 2 F2 ■ 1739 N St, NW ■ 202-785-1277 ■ www.tabardinn.com ■ $
A boutique hotel, named for the inn in Chaucer's *Canterbury Tales*, this is converted from three townhouses. The rooms are charming and eclectic, and most have private baths. The restaurant serves superb American-Continental cuisine; the lounge-bar has live jazz.

Churchill Hotel
MAP M1 ■ 1914 Connecticut Ave, NW ■ 202-797-2000 ■ www.the churchillhotel.com ■ $$
Opened as the Highlands apartment building in 1906, this grand Beaux Arts hotel in the Dupont Circle neighborhood, provides huge rooms.

Henley Park Hotel
MAP Q3 ■ 926 Massachusetts Ave, NW ■ 202-638-5200 ■ www.henleypark.com ■ $$
This Tudor-manor-style hotel boasts gargoyles on the outside and original stained glass and antique furniture inside.

Kimpton Morrison House
116 S Alfred St, Alexandria ■ 703-838-8000 ■ www.morrison house.com ■ $$
Recently redecorated, this trendy Federal-style hotel in the center of Old Town offers upscale accommodations while retaining the sophisticated historic details. The parlor and library are charming, and the onsite restaurant, Ashlar, offers locally sourced American fare.

Morrison-Clark Inn
MAP P3 ■ 1011 L St, NW ■ 202-898-1200 ■ www.morrisonclark.com ■ $$
Created by merging two townhouses, this mansion was the Soldiers, Sailors, Marines, and Airmen's Club for 50 years. Some of the original decorative touches still remain.

Renaissance Mayflower Hotel
MAP N3 ■ 1127 Connecticut Ave, NW ■ 202-347-3000 ■ www.renaissancemayflower.com ■ $$
Opened in 1925 on the day of Calvin Coolidge's presidential inauguration, this hotel has hosted every Inaugural Ball since. Harry S. Truman stayed here during White House renovations; Franklin D. Roosevelt wrote his 1933 inaugural address here; and J. Edgar Hoover had lunch here most days.

Hay-Adams Hotel
MAP N3 ■ 16th and H Sts, NW ■ 202-638-6600 ■ www.hayadams.com ■ $$$
Constructed on the sites of the homes of John Hay and Henry Adams, this elegant hotel features beautifully restored rooms furnished with antiques and ornamental ceilings. The Hays-Adams has stunning views.

The Jefferson
MAP N2 ■ 16th & M Sts, NW ■ 202-448-2300 ■ www.jeffersondc.com ■ $$$
The Jefferson's Beaux Arts facade is particularly eye-catching. The public areas feature displays of historic prints, paintings, and documents, including some associated with Thomas Jefferson. This elegant hotel is a popular choice with celebrities.

Phoenix Park Hotel
MAP R4 ■ 520 N Capitol St, NW ■ 202-638-6900 ■ www.phoenixparkhotel.com ■ $$$
Named after the iconic park in Dublin, this hotel, set in a stately 1920s Georgian Revival building, has an Irish theme, right down to the live music and house ales at the in-house pub.

St. Regis Hotel
MAP N2 ■ 923 16th St, NW ■ 202-638-2626 ■ www.stregiswashingtondc.com ■ $$$
If both Queen Elizabeth II and the Rolling Stones chose to stay here, the St. Regis must be doing something right. Calvin Coolidge took part in the 1926 opening of this grand hotel, styled after a Renaissance palace and beautifully appointed with antiques, chandeliers, and fine tapestries.

W Washington, DC

MAP P4 ■ 515 15th St, NW ■ 202-661-2400 ■ www. washingtondc.com ■ $$$

The city's historic Hotel Washington is now Hotel W, a prestigious property of Starwood Resorts and Hotels. Many of its rooms have superb views of the White House and other major landmarks. It offers exceptional service.

Willard InterContinental

MAP P4 ■ 1401 Pennsylvania Ave, NW ■ 202-628-9100 ■ www. washington.inter continental.com ■ $$$

This is undoubtedly among the most historic of the city's grand hotels. Momentous world events, including the birth of the League of Nations, were discussed here by leading figures, and royalty from all over the world have been its guests.

Luxury Hotels

Fairmont Washington DC

MAP M2 ■ 2401 M St, NW ■ 202-429-2400 ■ www. fairmont.com/washington ■ $$

The garden courtyard here is gorgeous, and there's a great pool and gym area, plus business facilities. Some of the Fairmont's rooms include delightful balconies.

Gaylord National Resort and Convention Center

MAP D6 ■ 201 Waterfront St, National Harbor, MD ■ 301-965-4000 ■ www. gaylordhotels.com ■ $$

The Gaylord National is the largest combined hotel and convention center on the East Coast. The soaring 18-storey glass atrium offers great views of the Potomac River and Alexandria.

The Graham Hotel

MAP 2 D3 ■ 1075 Thomas Jefferson St, NW ■ 202-337-0900 ■ www.the grahamgeorgetown.com ■ $$

The Graham offers its guests every luxury in the heart of Georgetown, with spacious, tranquil suites and a roof-deck bar.

Grand Hyatt Washington

MAP P3 ■ 1000 H St, NW ■ 202-582-1234 ■ www. grandhyattwashington. com ■ $$

The location of the Grand Hyatt is superb and its airy atrium is a spacious, attractive space with an adjacent Starbucks Reserve and the inviting Cure Bar & Bistro.

Hyatt Regency Washington on Capitol Hill

MAP R4 ■ 400 New Jersey Ave at D St, NW ■ 202-737-1234 ■ hyattregency washington.com ■ $$

This bustling hotel takes up an entire city block. It is conveniently set within easy walking distance of the US Capitol and the Smithsonian Museum.

Loews Madison Hotel

MAP P3 ■ 1177 15th St, NW ■ 202-862-1600 ■ www.loewshotels.com/ madison ■ $$

Located close to the White House, this chic hotel provides comfortable guestrooms, some with covered terraces. It also offers its guests free Wi-Fi throughout.

The Fairfax

MAP M2 ■ 2100 Massachusetts Ave, NW ■ 202-293-2100 ■ www. fairfaxwashingtondc.com ■ $$$

The Georgian-style decor here is complemented by large LCD TVs and DVD players. The hotel attracts diplomats, and celebrities looking for discretion. A concierge and a fitness room are available 24 hours a day.

Four Seasons Hotel

MAP L3 ■ 2800 Pennsylvania Ave, NW ■ 202-342-0444 ■ www. fourseasons.com/ washington ■ $$$

This is one of DC's best five-star hotels. The spa is renowned, and the hotel's Bourbon Steak restaurant is one of the best in the city. It's convenient for Georgetown and Rock Creek Park.

Mandarin Oriental Washington, DC

MAP P5 ■ 1330 Maryland Ave, SW ■ 202-554-8588 ■ www.mandarinoriental. com ■ $$$

Monumental views over the Potomac Tidal Basin and Jefferson Memorial are to be had at this elegant hotel. Rooms boast king beds and silk tapestries. There's also a spa, fitness center, and pool.

Park Hyatt Washington

MAP M2 ■ 24th St at M St, NW ■ 202-789-1234 ■ www.washingtondcpark. hyatt.com ■ $$$

The decor at this hotel features original moden artwork enhancing its elegant ambience. The hotel has an skylit indoor pool and a fitness center.

The Ritz-Carlton
MAP M3 ▪ 1150 22nd St, NW ▪ 202-835-0500 ▪ www.ritzcarlton.com ▪ $$$
The Ritz-Carlton provides the finest quality furnishings, including Egyptian cotton sheets and down comforters. The marble bathrooms are luxurious. Pool and spa facilities.

Boutique Hotels

Hotel Lombardy
MAP N3 ▪ 2019 Pennsylvania Ave, NW ▪ 202-828-2600 ▪ www.hotellombardy.com ▪ $$
This hotel is decorated with imported fabrics, Oriental rugs, and original art. The Cafe Lombardy restaurant is bistro-style.

Hotel Madera
MAP N2 ▪ 1310 New Hampshire Ave, NW ▪ 202-296-7600 ▪ www.hotelmadera.com ▪ $$
Offering modern comfort with a stylish twist, this small hotel exudes elegance and sophistication.

Hotel Monaco
MAP Q4 ▪ 700 F St, NW ▪ 202-628-7177 ▪ www.monaco-dc.com ▪ $$
Set in the 19th-century General Post Office building, the hotel has a stately facade and a colorful, modern interior. Upscale library bar for after-hours.

Hotel Palomar
MAP M2 ▪ 2121 P St, NW ▪ 202-448-1800 ▪ www.hotelpalomar-dc.com ▪ $$
This boutique hotel offers luxury accommodations in a lively neighborhood. Some rooms have spa-style bathrooms. Outdoor pool and sundeck.

Melrose Hotel
MAP M3 ▪ 2430 Pennsylvania Ave, NW ▪ 202-955-6400 ▪ www.melrosehoteldc.com ▪ $$
A modern hotel in the heart of town, the Melrose is known for its refined luxury. The furnishings are contemporary but with classic influences.

Sofitel Lafayette Square
MAP P3 ▪ 806 15th St, NW ▪ 202-730-8800 ▪ www.sofitel-washington-dc.com ▪ $$
On a corner of Lafayette Square, this 1862 building, transformed by the French Sofitel chain into an elegant hotel, has a gentleman's club-like ambience. The sound-proofing and acoustic doors are a welcome feature. The restaurant serves contemporary French bistro cuisine.

Topaz Hotel
MAP N2 ▪ 1733 N St, NW ▪ 202-393-3000 ▪ www.topazhotel.com ▪ $$
Located in a quiet corner of the Dupont Circle area, this hotel offers complimentary yoga mats and public bikes. The bar is among the best in the city.

University Inn Washington DC
MAP M3 ▪ 824 New Hampshire Ave, NW ▪ 202-780-8905 ▪ www.universityinndc.com ▪ $$
The handsome, large guest rooms and suites of this inn are colonial-inspired, but each come equipped with a refrigerator, a microwave, and a coffee-maker. Some even have kitchens. The Metro station and Kennedy Center are nearby.

The Hotel George
MAP R4 ▪ 15 E St, NW ▪ 202-347-4200 ▪ www.hotelgeorge.com ▪ $$$
One of the most chic hotels in Washington, deserving the attention because of its innovative design and excellent business facilities. The Bistro-style restaurant features French inspired dishes created by James Beard-award-winning chef Jeffrey Buben.

Rosewood Washington DC
MAP M3 ▪ 1050 31st St, NW ▪ 202-617-2400 ▪ www.rosewoodhotels.com ▪ $$$
Located along the C&O Canal in the heart of historic Georgetown, this elegant 49-room hotel offers a blend of old-world elegance and modern interiors.

Business Hotels

Courtyard Washington Convention Center
MAP Q4 ▪ 900 F St, NW ▪ 202-638-4600 ▪ www.courtyard.com/wascn ▪ $
Situated in a former 1891 bank but completely up to date, and with an indoor pool and fitness center. The hotel has two conference rooms.

Crystal City Marriott at Reagan National Airport
MAP D4 ▪ 1999 Jefferson Davis Highway, Arlington VA ▪ 703-413-5500 ▪ www.marriott.com ▪ $
This hotel has excellent business amenities and is close to Reagan airport. There are 13 meeting rooms and a walkway to a shopping mall.

Embassy Suites – Georgetown

MAP M2 ▪ 1250 22nd St, NW ▪ 202-857-3388 ▪ www.washingtondc. embassysuites.com ▪ $

Part of the Hilton Group, Embassy Suits offers well-furnished bedrooms with separate living areas. Conference rooms with extensive equipment are available for rent. There's also an indoor swimming pool and fitness center.

Hamilton Crowne Plaza Hotel

MAP P3 ▪ 14th and K St, NW ▪ 202-682-0111 ▪ www.hamiltonhoteldc. com ▪ $

This is a distinguished hotel, where the guest rooms offer a desk with high-speed internet and voicemail, and cable TV with in-room movies. Pets are welcome.

Capital Hilton

MAP N3 ▪ 1001 16th St at K St, NW ▪ 202-393-1000 ▪ www.hilton.com ▪ $$

This hotel is in a great location, just two blocks from the White House, and offers all the usual facilities offered by the Hilton chain, plus a health club and spa.

The Liaison Capitol Hill

MAP R4 ▪ 415 New Jersey Ave, NW ▪ 202-638-1616 ▪ www.jdvhotels.com ▪ $$

An elegant business boutique hotel with bright, contemporary styling, an inviting rooftop pool and patio, and the farm-fresh, southern inspired cuisine of Art and Soul bistro. The Liaison Capitol Hill is a popular hotel with upscale visitors.

Washington Hilton

MAP N1 ▪ 1919 Connecticut Ave, NW ▪ 202-483-3000 ▪ www. washington.hilton.com ▪ $$

The garden setting is lovely, and the elevated location gives a fine view of the city skyline. The complex's layout and size and its rooftop pool and sun deck make for a resort-like atmosphere.

Marriott Wardman Park

MAP J5 ▪ 2660 Woodley Rd, NW ▪ 202-328-2000 ▪ www.marriott.com ▪ $$$

Close to Rock Park Creek, this is the largest convention hotel in Washington. It combines charm with technology. It has scores of meeting rooms and an exhibition area. The well-maintained rooms offer all business services.

One Washington Circle Hotel

MAP M3 ▪ 1 Washington Circle, NW ▪ 202-872-1680 ▪ www.thecirclehotel.com ▪ $$$

Business travelers receive great service at this Foggy Bottom hotel. A knowledgeable staff manages the five meeting rooms, and suites have lots of seating space. Larger suites have full kitchens and walk-out balconies.

Washington Court Hotel

MAP 4 E3 ▪ 525 New Jersey Ave, NW ▪ 628-2100 ▪ www.washington courthotel.com ▪ $$$

The guest rooms at this hotel are sleek and modern, with free Wi-Fi and flatscreen TVs. Some have stunning views of the US Capitol.

The Westin Georgetown

MAP 2 E2 ▪ 2350 M St NW, 20037 ▪ 202-429-0100 ▪ www.westin georgetown.com ▪ $$$

Marble bathrooms with extra-deep bathtubs are among the amenities here. There is an outdoor pool and a leafy courtyard garden, with a choice of the Caucus Room French brasserie or the Latin-American Bóveda tavern for in-house dining. Dogs are permitted.

The Westin Washington DC City Center

MAP 3 B2 ▪ 1400 M St NW ▪ 429-1700 ▪ www. westinwashingtondc citycenter.com ▪ $$$

A large hotel with great weekend special deals, two full-service restaurants, plus an on-site Starbucks. Four blocks from the McPherson Metro, the Westin has a large central atrium and all the amenities one would expect for a largely business clientele. The hotel also provides a 24-hour fitness center, and is pet-friendly.

Family-Friendly Hotels

The Avenue Suites Georgetown

MAP M3 ▪ 2500 Pennsylvania Ave, NW ▪ 202-333-8060 ▪ www. avenuesuitesgeorge town.com ▪ $

This excellent Georgetown location provides a 24-hour gym, generous living rooms, large TVs, high-speed internet, and a fully equipped kitchen including a dishwasher. Pets are allowed.

For a key to hotel price categories see p126

Fairfield Inn and Suites

MAP Q3 ■ 500 H St, NW ■ 202-289-5959 ■ www. marriott.com ■ $

Formerly the Red Roof Inn, this hotel has been revamped by the Marriott chain and is now geared more to the business traveler. However, prices are still reasonable, the staff are great, and the suites are a good choice for family stays. The hotel is within easy reach of the Capital One Arena.

Hampton Inn and Suites National Harbor/Alexandria Area

MAP C5 ■ 250 Waterfront Street, Oxon Hill, MD ■ 301-567-3531 ■ www. hamptoninn.com ■ $

Located just a block away from the Potomac river with a carousel and a giant Ferris wheel set two blocks away, the Hampton Inn & Suites is very child-friendly. Amenities here include an indoor pool, free hot breakfast, and Wi-Fi. The location is handy for exploring Mount Vernon and historic Old Town Alexandria.

Holiday Inn Central

MAP P2 ■ 1501 Rhode Island Ave at 15th St, NW ■ 202-483-2000 ■ www. inndc.com ■ $

This hotel located in downtown Washington has a rooftop pool, cable TV, and in-room movies that will keep children entertained. Some over-sized rooms are available for families. The Dupont Circle and McPherson Square Metro stops are located within walking distance of the hotel.

Holiday Inn Capitol

MAP Q5 ■ 550 C St, SW ■ 202-479-4000 ■ www. hicapitoldc.com ■ $$

This Holiday Inn is a great choice for families – it offers an outdoor rooftop pool with a view; it is just one block away from the Air and Space Museum; and kids under 12 can eat for free. In addition, there is a Starbucks on-site. The hotel also provides guest laundry facilities.

Holiday Inn Hotel & Suites, Alexandria Old Town

MAP C5 ■ 625 First St, Alexandria VA ■ 703-548-6300 ■ www.ihg.com ■ $$

Located near the shops and restaurants of historic Old Town Alexandria, this pleasant outpost of the Holiday Inn chain is also well positioned for exploring Mount Vernon (the estate of George Washington), Arlington National Cemetery, and National Harbor. Children under 19 stay free in their parents' room. The hotel features indoor and outdoor pools, free Wi-Fi, and a continental breakfast for guests.

J.W. Marriott

MAP P4 ■ 1331 Pennsylvania Ave, NW ■ 202-393-2000■ www. marriott.com/wasjw ■ $$

Located only two blocks away from the White House and set close to the National Mall and the fun International Spy Museum, this hotel has a great location that minimizes walking distances for little feet. Childcare is also offered by prior arrangement. A fitness center is also available. Free Wi-Fi in public areas.

Omni Shoreham Hotel

MAP J5 ■ 2500 Calvert St, NW (at Connecticut Ave) ■ 202-234-0700 ■ www. omnihotels.com ■ $$

Set close to Rock Creek Park and the National Zoo, the Omni Shoreham Hotel's location makes it ideal for travelers with children. All its young guests are provided with interesting activity backpacks on check-in.

Washington Plaza

MAP P2 ■ 10 Thomas Circle, NW ■ 202-842-1300 ■ www.washingtonplaza hotel.com ■ $$

The resort-like hotel and its beautifully landscaped grounds surround a large open-air swimming pool. There is poolside dining during the summer, and a lounge with an open fire during the winter.

Courtyard Washington, DC/ Dupont Circle

MAP M1 ■ 1900 Connecticut Ave, NW ■ 202-332-9300 ■ www. marriott.com ■ $$$

Conveniently located for the National Zoo, this hotel provides HDTV in all rooms, and a fresh food grab-and-go bistro in the lobby. The outdoor pool is safe for kids, and there are free cookies available every afternoon.

Hotel RL

MAP N3 ■ 1823 L St, NW ■ 202-223-4320 ■ www. redlion.com/washington-dc ■ $$$

Located downtown, this stylish contemporary hotel is two blocks away from the Metro and close to the White House. Guest rooms are spacious with convenient kitchenettes, Direct TV, flat screen TV and free Wi-Fi.

Mid-Priced Hotels

Windsor Inn

MAP N1 ▪ 1842 16th St, NW ▪ 202-667-0300 ▪ www.windsor-inn-hotel-dc.com ▪ $

Two 1920s buildings offer big-hotel amenities in a charming small-hotel environment. The main building is listed in the National Register of Historic Places, and has some marvelous Art Deco ornamentation. Free Wi-Fi and complimentary newspapers are available for guests.

Beacon Hotel and Corporate Quarters

MAP 3 B2 ▪ 1615 Rhode Island Ave, NW (at 17th St), 20036 ▪ 202-296-2100 ▪ www.beaconhotelwdc.com ▪ $$

The very comfortable rooms are decorated with cosmopolitan flair. Eight deluxe turret suites and 60 corporate suites come with fully equipped kitchens, high-speed internet and web TV. The Beacon Bar & Grill restaurant serves food throughout the day, from breakfast to dinner.

Capitol Hill Hotel

MAP S5 ▪ 200 C St, SE ▪ 202-543-6000 ▪ www.capitolhillhotel–dc.com ▪ $$

This suites-only hotel was re-created from an apartment building, and the result is generously spacious rooms with kitchens. It's located near the Library of Congress, the US Capitol, and Eastern Market.

Embassy Suites Hotel at the Chevy Chase Pavilion

4300 Military Rd, NW (at Wisconsin & Western Aves), 20015 ▪ 202-362-9300 ▪ www.embassysuitesdcmetro.com ▪ $$

Situated in the popular Chevy Chase shopping district, this all-suites hotel has easy access to a wide range of shops and restaurants, as well as the Friendship Heights Metro, all within the Chevy Chase Pavilion. Breakfast is included in the tariff, and complimentary drinks and appetizers are served at a two-hour reception in Willie's Bar every evening.

Georgetown Inn

MAP L2 ▪ 1310 Wisconsin Ave, NW ▪ 202-333-8900 ▪ www.georgetowninn.com ▪ $$

This hotel opened in 1961 at the height of John F. Kennedy's administration and the public's interest in Georgetown glamor, and it has been a fixture on the Washington hotel scene ever since. All rooms are large and decorated in tasteful, elegant style, and offer free Wi-Fi. The Executive Rooms have a sitting area that is large enough to hold a meeting in.

Georgetown Inn West End

MAP M3 ▪ 1121 New Hampshire Ave, NW ▪ 202-457-0565 ▪ georgetowninnwestend.com ▪ $$

With a location equidistant from the White House, historic Georgetown and the lively Dupont Circle neighborhood, this newly renovated boutique hotel is quickly becoming a

favorite with both families and businesspeople. A free continental breakfast is served daily. Children 17 and under stay free.

Georgetown Suites

MAP L3 ▪ 1111 30th St, NW ▪ 202-298-7800 ▪ www.georgetownsuites.com ▪ $$

Georgetown Suites offers its guests a wide variety of accommodations, ranging from studios to a two-bedroom penthouse with a private patio that has Potomac River views. All have a separate sitting area and kitchen, as well as free Wi-Fi.

The Normandy Hotel

MAP M1 ▪ 2118 Wyoming Ave, NW ▪ 202-483-1350 ▪ www.thenormandydc.com ▪ $$

Located on a peaceful residential street, the Normandy has the feel of a bed and breakfast. Complimentary wine and cheese are served to guests on Tuesday nights, and coffee, tea, and cookies are offered at other times.

Renaissance Washington, DC Downtown

MAP Q3 ▪ 999 9th St, NW ▪ 202-898-9000 ▪ www.marriot.com ▪ $$

This large hotel, with over 800 rooms, is hard to miss thanks to its striking glass facade. It may be oriented toward business travelers, but is set in an excellent tourist location in Penn Quarter. It also features full-service spas and business centers, a library in the lobby, and several dining options, including the Liberty Market deli.

For a key to hotel price categories see p126

Washington Marriott at Metro Center
MAP P3 ■ 775 12th St, NW ■ 202-737-2200 ■ www.marriott.com ■ $$
Benefitting greatly from its excellent downtown location, this smart, modern hotel provides guests with a personal touch despite its large size and 459 rooms and suites. The Fire and Sage restaurant serves seasonal food, and there is a pool and fitness center.

L'Enfant Plaza Hotel
MAP Q5 ■ 480 L'Enfant Plaza, SW ■ 202-484-1000 ■ www.hiltondcnationalmall.com ■ $$$
This member of the Hilton hotel chain is surrounded by over 40 upscale shops and restaurants and is close to the engaging and fun International Spy Museum. The contemporary decor is dazzling, and there are fine views of the National Mall.

Budget Hotels

Adams Inn
MAP D3 ■ 1746 Lanier Place, NW ■ 202-745-3600 ■ www.adamsinn.com ■ $
A charming urban inn, this is sprawled across three 100-year-old townhouses and boasts a very pretty garden. Some of the 27 rooms share a bathroom but have a sink in the bedroom; all have free Wi-Fi.

Days Inn
4400 Connecticut Ave NW, Van Ness, 20008 ■ 202-244-5600 ■ www.dcdaysinn.com ■ $
A convenient, affordable hotel, north of Cleveland Park near the Van Ness

Metro, with clean rooms. Several restaurants are located nearby, including the Tesoro next door, which serves authentic Italian cuisine.

The District Hotel
MAP P2 ■ 1440 Rhode Island Ave, NW ■ 202-232-7800 ■ www.districthotel.com ■ $
This charming historic building, about six blocks from the White House, has been converted into 58 comfortable rooms with private bath that are popular with travelers on a limited budget.

Embassy Inn
MAP N2 ■ 1627 16th St, NW ■ 202-234-7800 ■ www.embassy-inn-hotel-dc.com ■ $
An elegant apartment house built in 1910 has been converted into a small hotel with 38 guest rooms, all with private bath. The hotel has been modernized, but many of the original features still remain, as do the tasteful facade and entranceway. Rooms are furnished with reproduction antiques and all come with free Wi-Fi.

Homewood Suites
MAP P2 ■ 1475 Massachusetts Ave, NW ■ 202-265-8000 ■ www.homewood-suites.com ■ $
This 175-room member of the Hilton hotel group is ideal for extended stays as it is centrally located and offers good-sized accommodations, with separate living and sleeping areas and full kitchen. A free hot breakfast is served daily, and there are laundry facilities and a 24/7 convenience store.

Hotel Harrington
MAP P4 ■ 11th & E Sts, NW ■ 202-628-8140 ■ www.hotel-harrington.com ■ $
At one time, this was the largest hotel in the city. A century later, it is still run by members of the founding family. It is popular with school groups, and also has some family suites that have two bathrooms each.

State Plaza Hotel
MAP M4 ■ 2117 E St, NW ■ 202-861-8200 ■ www.stateplaza.com ■ $
This chic all-suites hotel, conveniently located between the White House and the Kennedy Center, features a bistro with outdoor seating, a rooftop sun deck, and a fitness center. Suites come with kitchens and have high-speed internet access.

The American Guest House
MAP F2 ■ 2005 Columbia Rd, NW ■ 202-588-1180 ■ www.americanguesthouse.com ■ $$
Set in a colonial-style townhouse dating from 1898, this charming guesthouse provides a comfortable base for travelers in the elegant Kalorama neighborhood. The 12 well-maintained rooms, with Wi-Fi, are handsomely furnished with wood floors, Oriental carpets, and period furnishings and artwork. A free homemade breakfast is offered daily.

The Donovan
MAP P3 ■ 1155 14th St, NW ■ 202-737-1200 ■ www.donovanhoteldc.com ■ $$
Located in the center of downtown Washington,

this hotel has a fantastic rooftop bar and pool that provide great city views. Rooms and public areas are stylishly chic, with a futuristic feel, and there's a hosted Wine Hour every evening. Its restaurant, Zentan, serves Japanese cuisine and a range of innovative cocktails.

The River Inn
MAP M3 ■ 924 25th St, NW ■ 202-337-7600 ■ www.theriverinn.com ■ $$
This popular hotel in Foggy Bottom has 126 suites, each with a full kitchen and a good-sized work or dining area. The hotel's name reflects its remarkable river views.

Bed and Breakfast

Akwaaba Bed & Breakfast
MAP N2 ■ 1708 16th St, NW ■ 866-466-3855 ■ www.akwaaba.com ■ $
This charming bed and breakfast is located within walking distance of the White House. The historic townhouse has eight ensuite rooms, featuring premium linens, cable TV, and free Wi-Fi. Some rooms have a private balcony, Jacuzzi tub, and a decorative fireplace.

Mt. Vernon Square Bed and Breakfast
MAP Q2 ■ 400 M St, NW 20001 ■ 888-399-5496 ■ www.mvsbb.com ■ $
A restored townhouse with clean, spacious and comfortable rooms. Walking distance from several restaurants, bars, clubs, the Smithsonian Museum, National Mall, and other sites. Ask for a quiet room as the traffic may bother some.

Taft Bridge Inn
MAP M1 ■ 2007 Wyoming Ave, NW ■ 202-387-2007 ■ www.taftbridgeinn.com ■ $
At this Inn, you'll find 12 beautifully decorated rooms in Victorian style. It's near the zoo and the vibrant Adams Morgan neighborhood, and a free breakfast is included.

Chester A. Arthur Bed and Breakfast
MAP P2 ■ 13th and P Sts, NW (at Logan Circle) ■ 202-328-3510 ■ www.chesterarthurhouse.com ■ $$
This handsome, elegantly restored 19th-century townhouse offers its guests oversized rooms with antiques, cable TV, and internet access.

Embassy Circle Guest House
MAP F3 ■ 2224 R St, NW ■ 202-232-7744 ■ www.dcinns.com ■ $$
Rated one of the best bed and breakfasts in the city, the Embassy Circle Guest House has 11 rooms, all with a private bath and shower. There are no TV sets or radios here, but there's plenty of entertainment available within a five-minute walk in the vibrant Dupont Circle neighborhood. A complimentary buffet breakfast is included in the rate.

The Inn at Dupont South
MAP N2 ■ 1312 19th St, NW ■ 202-359-8432 ■ www.thedupontcollection.com ■ $$
Set just south of Dupont Circle, the Inn at Dupont South occupies a Victorian row house dating to 1855. Most of the bedrooms have a private bath and fireplace, and all have air-conditioning and wireless internet access. There's a private walled garden in which to enjoy a relaxing afternoon tea.

Swann House
MAP N1 ■ 1808 New Hampshire Ave, NW ■ 202-265-4414 ■ www.swannhouse.com ■ $$
Sometimes described as the best bed and breakfast in the city, this inviting, well-appointed 1883 mansion combines sparkling chandeliers and open fireplaces with all modern conveniences – Wi-Fi, private baths, and cable TV, and even a pool. Breakfast includes their homemade granola and gourmet hot dishes.

Woodley Park Guest House
MAP C3 ■ 2647 Woodley Rd, NW ■ 202-667-0218 ■ www.dcinns.com ■ $$
This family-oriented bed and breakfast features airy, comfortable rooms, decorated with tasteful furnishings and collector art. The hearty buffet breakfast will keep everyone going till lunch at the nearby National Zoo. The National Cathedral and Metro are also close by.

Mansion on O Street
MAP N2 ■ 2020 O St, NW ■ 202-496-2000 ■ www.omansion.com ■ $$$
This inn offers a variety of themed rooms, including a Graceland suite filled with memorabilia and the James Bond suite hidden behind a secret door. The layout is so striking that guests often regard the house as a sight in itself. Eclectic and charming.

General Index

Page numbers in **bold**
refer to Top 10 highlights.

Acknowledgments

Author

Ron Burke is the author or co-author of 19 books. A former Capitol Hill resident, he was born in the Washington, DC metropolitan area and has lived here most of his life.

Susan Burke lives in Virginia, where she worked on a daily newspaper for 20 years before becoming an editor for the Air Line Pilots Association. She is also a freelance editor for journals on labor, economics, and art conservation.

Additional contributor
Paul Franklin, Nancy Mikula

Publishing Director Georgina Dee

Publisher Vivien Antwi

Design Director Phil Ormerod

Editorial Michelle Crane, Rebecca Flynn, Rachel Fox, Fay Franklin, Fíodhna Ní Ghríofa, Freddie Marriage, Scarlett O'Hara, Marianne Petrou, Sally Schafer, Christine Stroyan

Revisions Ankita Awasthi Tröger, Emma Brady, Neha Chander, Bhavika Mathur, Nancy Mikula, Alice Powers, Ankita Sharma, Aakanksha Singh, Rituraj Singh, Akanksha Siwach, Sumita Khatwani, Priyanka Thakur, Rachel Thompson

Design Richard Czapnik, Marisa Renzullo, Jaynan Spengler

Picture Research Phoebe Lowndes, Susie Peachey, Ellen Root, Oran Tarjan

Cartography Subhashree Bharti, Simonetta Giori, Suresh Kumar, Casper Morris, John Plumer

DTP Jason Little, George Nimmo, Azeem Siddiqui, Joanna Stenlake

Production Nancy-Jane Maun

Factchecker Alice Powers

Proofreader Alyson Silverwood

Indexer Hilary Bird

Illustrator Chris Orr & Associates

First edition produced by Sargasso Media Ltd, London

Commissioned Photography: Paul Franklin, Rough Guides/Angus Osborn, Rough Guides/Paul Whitfield, Kim Sayer, Giles Stokoe

Picture Credits

Popperfoto 44cb; Tim Sloan 12bl; Chip Somodevilla 67tr; Daniel Stein 64tl; Julie Thurston Photography 80b; Universal Images Group 44tl; The Washington Post 67cl, 73cl, / Bill O'Leary 90br; Alex Wong 16bl.

John Fluevog Shoes/Raw Information Group: 108tr.

Kramerbooks & Afterwords Cafe & Grill: Kate Headley 114tr.

Mary Evans Picture Library: Everett Collection 14br.

Monocle: Gary Hopkins 83tr.

NASA: Landsat 8 20tr.

Courtesy of the National Gallery of Art, Washington: The Jolly Flatboatmen, George Caleb Bingham, 1846, National Gallery of Art, Washington, Patrons' Permanent Fund 24bl; George Washington portrait c.1850 by Rembrandt Peale, Gift of Mr. and Mrs. George W. Davison 14c; The Adoration of the Magi, Fra Angelico e. 1395-1455, Lippi, Filippo, Fra c. 1406–1469. tempera on panel, 137.3 cm (54 1/16 in.) Samuel H. Kress Collection1952.2.2 / 24cla; Right and Left, 1909, Winslow Homer, 1836–1910, oil on canvas, 71.8 x 122.9 cm (28 1/4 x 48 3/8 in.) Gift of the Avalon Foundation 25tl; George Washington c. 1803/1805, Gilbert Stuart 1755–1828. oil on canvas 73.6 x 61.4 cm (29 x 24 3/16 in.) Gift of Jean McGinley Draper 1954 9.2.25cra; The Dance Lesson c 1879, Edgar Degas. oil on canvas. 38 x 88 cm (14 15/16 x 34 5/8 in.) Collection of Mr. and Mrs. Paul Mellon 26t; Sculpture garden featuring Graft, Roxy Paine 27b; 'Symphony in White, No. 1: The White Girl' 1862, James McNeill Whistler 1834–1903, oil on canvas, 213 x 107.9 cm, Harris Whittemore Collection 89tr.

Courtesy of the National Park Service: Abbie Row 19b.

National Museum of African American History and Culture: 55cr.

National Museum of American History/ Smithsonian Institution: 10br; 22bl, 22cra 23clb.

Restaurant Eve: 115crb.

Smithsonian's National Zoo: 33tl, 70t.

West End Bistro: 68clb.

White House Collection, Copyright White House Historical Association: Peter Vitale 16crb, 17cr, 17br, 18tl, 18cr, 18bc

Cover images

Front & spine – **Getty Images:** Visions Of Our Land. Back – **4Corners:** Massimo Borchi.

Pull out map cover

Getty Images: Visions Of Our Land

All other images are: © Dorling Kindersley. For further information see www.dkimages.com.

Key to abbreviations in visitor information blocks:
Adm = admission charge.

Penguin Random House

Printed and bound in China

First published in Great Britain in 2003 by Dorling Kindersley Limited 80 Strand, London WC2R 0RL

Copyright 2003, 2018 © Dorling Kindersley Limited

A Penguin Random House Company

18 19 20 21 10 9 8 7 6 5 4 3 2 1

Reprinted with revisions 2004, 2005, 2006, 2007, 2008, 2010, 2011, 2012, 2013, 2014, 2016 (twice), 2017, 2018

Published in Great Britain by Dorling Kindersley Limited.

A CIP catalogue record is available from the British Library.

ISBN 978-0-2413-1164-6

MIX
Paper from responsible sources
FSC™ C018179

SPECIAL EDITIONS OF DK TRAVEL GUIDES

Selected Street Index